The Homebrewer's Garden

How to easily grow,
prepare and use your own
Hops • Brewing Herbs • Malts

Joe Fisher and Dennis Fisher

Storey Publishing

The mission of Storey Publishing is to serve our customers by publishing practical information that encourages personal independence in harmony with the environment.

Edited by Brad Ring
Cover design by Rob Johnson, Rob Johnson Design
Cover photographs © StockFood: Foster (center),
Martina Meuth (top left), Zabert Sandmann (top)
Text design and production by Mark Tomasi
Line drawings by Sarah Brill, except for those by Cathy Baker (pages 26-28);
Beverly Duncan (pages 67, 69, 72, 85, 88, and 89); Judy Eliason (page 99);
Brigita Fuhrmann (pages 53, 62, 73, 80, 81, 84, 92, 95, 98, and 104);
Charles Joslin (page 96); and Mallory Lake (pages 76, 91, 94, and 102)
Indexed by Nan Badgett, Word•a•bil•i•ty

Printed in the United States by Versa Press

20   19   18   17

Library of Congress Cataloging-in-Publication Data

Fisher, Joe, 1966–
    The homebrewer's garden : how to easily grow, prepare, and use your
own hops, brewing herbs, malts / Joe Fisher and Dennis Fisher.
        p.   cm.
    Includes bibliographical references (p.   -   ) and index.
    ISBN 978-1-58017-010-9 (pbk. : alk. paper)
    1. Brewing—Amateur's manuals. 2. Hops. 3. Herbs. 4. Malt.
    I. Fisher, Dennis, 1963–   . II. Title.
TP570.F543   1998
641.8'73—dc21   98-19169
                                                                CIP

Table of Contents

Dedication

To Poppa Donald and Gram Ruth

Acknowledgements

Many people helped us in the research of this book. We would especially like to thank Dena Nishek, formerly of *Zymurgy* magazine; Walter K. Wornick of the American Heather Society; Susan Yusishen of Performance Seeds Ltd.; Gordon Gowlett of Maris Otter; Murray McLelland of Alberta Agriculture; Professor William TeBrake; John Bunker of Fedco Seeds; Brad and Caitlin Hunter of Appleton Creamery; Tina Roberts and Steve Peary; Rani Cross of Skyscraper Hill Organic Gardens; Sumner and Paula Roberts of Meadowsweet Farm; Matt Williams; Dana and Mark Llewellyn of Apple Hill Farms; Ben Gleason, Scott Nelson, and Don Wagoner; Pamela Lappies; our parents, and Sue.

The Advantages of Growing Your Own

HOMEBREWERS today can buy most of what they need in homebrew supply stores, and this is a great convenience for all concerned. But if you have a little land, or even a sunny porch, you can grow enough of your own hops, herbs, and adjuncts to make a real contribution to the flavor, aroma, and uniqueness of your homebrew. Everything you need to make beer can be grown in garden-sized plots, including grains for malting. And even if you grow nothing at all, we can still show you how to find and use a variety of unusual brewing ingredients.

We've found that one of the most satisfying aspects of homebrewing is producing some or all of your own brewing ingredients from scratch. Not surprisingly, this is called *scratch brewing*. The term refers to the cultivation, preparation, and use of hops, barley malts and other nonbarley grains, and adjuncts ranging from herbs to fruits and vegetables.

The reasons for growing your own are many. First of all, it gives you a tremendous amount of control over what does and what doesn't go into your beer. That's important to a lot of people. You can be as organic as you want when growing your own products, confident in the knowledge that they haven't been sprayed with something poisonous at some point in their growth.

Secondly, you can improve the quality of your beer by using your own ingredients. This is a point we can't make strongly enough. *Homegrown ingredients are the best ingredients for beer; the more you use, the better your beer will be.* You will know that your hops, herbs, malts, and other ingredients are at their peak of freshness if you are in charge of their growing, harvesting, drying, and storage. You will also find that having a backlog of brewing ingredients is a great incentive to brew more beer.

Thirdly, you will have access to varieties of ingredients that you just can't get anywhere else. That makes you more self-sufficient. You will also be able to produce your own ingredients less expensively than you could buy them. By combining home hop growing with home malting and yeast culturing, you actually can get the cost of brewing a batch of fine all-grain beer below the price of a six-pack of cheap commercial brew! If you're interested in yeast culturing, Roger Leistad's book *Yeast Culturing for the Homebrewer* (G.W. Kent, 1983) is a good resource. Even if you can save just a dollar or so per batch of beer, it will make a big difference in the long run.

Fourthly, home growing puts you in touch with the history of brewing and opens up new avenues for experimentation. Both are goals for many homebrewers. Beyond simple historical interest, there are plenty of herbs and other little-used adjuncts out there that make great beer. People have just forgotten how to use them.

And finally, it's fun. And let's not underestimate the value of having a good time in homebrewing. It's great to enter contests and win ribbons. It's also nice to save money over pricey microbrews and imports (up to *one thousand percent* if you compare the cost of a batch of simple homebrewed bitter made with purchased ingredients to the cost of a glass of beer in a brewpub). But if you aren't having fun, what's the point?

We became interested in scratch brewing years ago when we realized how many of the things we grew in our gardens could be used in beer. Mainly we were thinking about *adjuncts,* extras like pumpkin in pumpkin ale, the herbs in herb beer or the honey in honey lager. Later we got interested in growing the staples of beermaking, the grains and hops.

Gardening and brewing are two highly complementary disciplines. Both require intelligence, patience, independent mindedness (which homebrewers have by the barrelful), respect for the craft, and a willingness to experiment and to learn. Plus, the products of each can be used in the other: Herbs, fruit, grains, and so forth go into beer, and you can recycle brewing residues in your garden. Nothing is wasted. The growth of interest in gardening, especially in growing old-fashioned or heirloom varieties of plants instead of hybrids, is part of the same search for quality that is fueling the growth of homebrewing and microbrewing.

The purpose of this book is not to make your life more complicated. We have tried to keep things as simple as possible, which is why there is an emphasis on extract or partial-mash brewing. In our experience this is how most people brew, and it's how we tend to do things ourselves, with only occasional forays into more rarified kinds of brewing. All-grain brewing, making your own beer from grain without the use of any extracts, is a fascinating science. But it requires a certain level of expertise and, generally speaking, a lot of equipment. It also takes a lot of time compared to brewing from extracts, and not everyone has that kind of time to invest in beer.

We've tried to include topics that will be useful to people at every level of brewing. For the intermediate homebrewer, growing your own is an opportunity to expand your brewing horizons without necessarily taking the plunge into all-grain brewing. It's easy enough for the advanced brewer to convert some of our extract or partial-mash recipes to all-grain recipes.

You may be more interested in hops than in other kinds of herbs. We'll tell you where to find hop rhizomes, where to plant them, how to tend them, and how to harvest and use the hop flowers. Or you may want to learn about malting, but not about growing grain. We tell you how to locate various types of grain and what to do with them once you've found them. And we provide recipes using homemade grains, homegrown hops, herbs, and adjuncts.

People brew beer for a lot of reasons, but the two most important things to do in homebrewing are to enjoy yourself and to make beer that you like. *The Homebrewer's Garden* will help you do both.

Homegrown Hops

"Because it is easy to grow, so they should be in every garden; every landowner should devote a small area to them sufficiently large to allow in a good hop year enough hops to be grown for his own house brewery."

— Johannes Gottfried Hahn, *Die Hausbrauerei,* **1804**

THIS advice still sounds good today. Hops are a versatile crop that can be grown for both ornamental and practical purposes. They are attractive plants that make great arbors, wreaths, arrangements — and of course beer. Every homebrewer who owns a piece of land should try his or her hand at growing a few hop vines.

When you grow your own hops, you can pick them at their absolute peak of readiness. As soon as hops are picked, they start to lose the essential oils needed for good flavor and aroma. The best way to know that your hops haven't been sitting on a shelf for a year is to grow your own. Commercial whole hops, the least processed form available, have been cut down, run through a picking machine, dried, baled, shipped, repackaged, and shipped again before reaching your homebrew store. Inevitably, some of the hops' bitter resins and essential oils are lost during processing. Your own hops will never have to run that gauntlet, making them fresher, more aromatic, and better for brewing than any you could buy. Homegrown hops have a fresh earthiness that adds a delicious immediacy to the beer drinking experience. The aroma alone will be enough to convert you, to say nothing of the flavor.

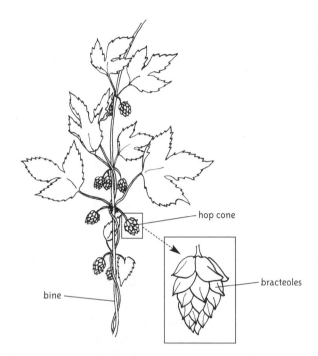

You can also save money growing your own hops. Once the initial investment of a few dollars per plant is made and you've bought your trellis materials, there will be few other expenses beyond the time you spend tending the plants. For an average batch of beer, you can spend three dollars just for the hops in a homebrew store. This translates into a fair amount of money if you brew frequently. You can dramatically reduce this bill and even eliminate it altogether, if you're willing to go to the trouble of growing all of your own bittering and aroma hops.

The best reason of all to grow hops may be a spiritual one. A fine, lush trellis of the green, prickly vines, heavy with hop flowers, says as well as anything else that you are a serious homebrewer. And believe us, your guests will be extremely impressed when you tell them that you grew the hops in the beer they're drinking.

Humulus lupulus: The Friendly Hop

Cultivating hops is easy; all they really need is reasonably fertile soil, plenty of sunlight and moisture, and something to climb on. Hops are so vigorous, in fact, that their tendency to run wild in cultivated fields is commemorated in the second part of their botanical name: *Lupulus* means "wolflike."

The cone blossoms of the female vine are the part that home-brewers are concerned about. They contain lupulin, a yellowish powder that contains the bitter resins and essential oils that give beer its flavor and aroma.

HOP FACTS

▸ Anatomy — There are both male and female hop plants, but for beer making only the female is important. Females produce scaly cones about 1 inch (2.5 cm) long that are loaded with lupulin, a yellow powder that contains the bitter resins and essential oils that give beer its flavor. The cones hang in clusters. The "petals" on the cone are called *bracteoles* and hide the lupulin glands. The coiling green vines are also called *bines* — the botanical term for twining vines. The vines are covered with a thick growth of large, spiky leaves shaped something like cucumber leaves. The vines grow from thick rhizomes, which are underground stems that look like fat roots. The entire root-and-rhizome structure is called a crown. New hop plants are usually grown from rhizomes divided off other hop crowns.

▸ Properties — The hop plant (botanical name: *Humulus lupulus*) is a vining perennial, meaning its vines will grow year after year from the same roots if cared for properly. The plant has a very vigorous growth habit, sending up long, spiny shoots that can reach up to 30 feet (9 m) in height. The plant can tolerate poor soil but grows best in rich ground and is hardy to Zone 3. It likes moisture and plenty of sun. The rhizomes spread underground almost as fast as the vines do aboveground. Vines need regular pruning each year, and even the rhizomes benefit from root pruning every three years. Hop vines require a strong, permanent structure to support them, such as a trellis or pergola.

Choosing Which Hop Varieties to Grow

If you live in a major hop-producing area, such as the Pacific Northwest, you can probably get hops directly from a nearby commercial grower. Otherwise you can order hop plants from one of the sources listed in appendix B, or get them from a homebrew store. Some seed catalogs now offer hops as a novelty item, but they usually don't identify the variety.

Hop rhizomes are available from most well-stocked homebrew stores in early spring. Usually they will be large, lumpy roots about a foot long; depending on how the grower has trimmed them, they could be as short as a few inches.

The rhizomes you buy are all female, because the hops used in beer are the flowers of the female hop plant. If you get a male plant by accident, it will be easy to tell as soon as it blooms: Male blossoms look like typical flowers, not like green hop cones. Male plants should be returned to the supplier because they're useless for making beer. Hop rhizomes usually cost less than five dollars each, cheap when you consider that you'll never have to buy any again unless you want more varieties.

HOP RHIZOME CHECKLIST

Appearance
- ✓ Plump, not dried out or withered
- ✓ Healthy, not dead- or diseased-looking
- ✓ May have new white sprouts and rootlets

Texture
- ✓ Firm to the touch, no soft spots
- ✓ Will not compress easily

Care until Planting
- ✓ Keep in a cool, damp place; wrap in newspaper, damp sawdust, or peat moss to prevent drying out

Experimenting with Different Varieties

Your homebrew store owner will probably be able to recommend which hops will grow best in your region, or at least put you in touch with other local growers.

A good rule for growing hops (or any other kind of plant) is: "If it can't live like we do, we don't want it." If a particular variety grows up looking sickly, with brown leaves and flowers, or is constantly attacked by insects or diseases, dig it up and try something different. For this reason you shouldn't plant rhizomes of only a single variety the first year, even if you prefer a particular kind of hop. Other varieties may do better in your area, and you don't want to waste a lot of time and effort caring for plants that would rather be growing somewhere else. Unhealthy plants won't produce good yields, so get plants that like your land.

Grow at least three or four different kinds to start. Watch how they perform and keep the varieties that do the best. Health is the top priority; other hop qualities are really secondary when you are growing your own. Your hops may have very different characteristics than the ones of the same variety you buy in the store, because climate, soil composition, altitude, and other factors will influence your crops to some degree. This difference can result in some highly individual beers.

HOOK UP WITH LOCAL HOP GROWERS

Getting rhizomes and advice from local growers is the best method we know to start out right with your hop growing, for three reasons. First, you already know that the hop variety they are growing will do well in your region. Second, you can get firsthand growing tips. Finally, most hobbyists offer rhizomes for free. Ask your homebrew store or fellow homebrewers for leads to track down backyard hop growers near you. If you live in the United States and don't know of any homebrewers living near you, you can contact the American Homebrewers Association for a list of clubs in your region. Their phone number is (303) 447-0816.

START SMALL

You shouldn't get overambitious the first year. Grow one row of hops rather than six. If you live in a good area for hop growing, and you have the land and the time, you can probably grow most if not all of the hops you will need for homebrewing. But no matter where you live, you should get into hop growing gradually. It's better to have a few hop plants and tend them carefully to achieve good yields than to have dozens with rank growth and few cones.

When choosing which hops to grow, bear in mind your location and how long a harvest season you want. If your area has a short growing season, you should grow hops that mature early. If you have a longer growing season and want to stretch out your harvest, combine early hops with some that mature later. As a general rule, German and Czechoslovakian style aromatic lager hops don't produce as well in North America as ale-type hops (for some exceptions, see Fuggles and Perle). You may notice that we don't include specific *alpha acid* percentages for each hop variety in our chart. That's because alpha acids are not an absolute value — they vary from crop to crop, year to year, and place to place. As a rule, alpha acid percentages are higher within the same varieties for homegrown hops than for commercially available hops. We should also note that when a hop variety that you purchase at a homebrew store has a place name before it (for example, B.C. Goldings and East Kent Goldings), it indicates where the hop was grown and not a different variety. In this case, B.C. Goldings are from British Columbia, Canada, while the East Kent Goldings hops are grown in England. Since geography plays a large role in a hop's final characteristics, these Goldings will differ just as the hops you grow in your backyard won't turn out exactly like the store-bought varieties you are used to using.

Variety	Characteristics	Cone Style	Yield	Ready for Harvest
Brewer's Gold	A traditional bittering hop from England with poor aroma. Similar to Bullion, but more resistant to disease. Healthy grower.	Medium, tight cones	High	Midseason
Bullion	English hop with moderate bitterness, no aroma, and an interesting blackberry flavor. Vigorous grower. Somewhat resistant to disease.	Large, tight cones	High	Late season
Cascade	Spicy flavor and citrus aroma. Vigorous grower.	Elongated cones	High	Midseason
Centennial	Like Cascade but more bitter; floral aroma and spicy flavor. Vigorous grower.	Medium, tight cones	Moderate	Midseason
Chinook	Very bitter. Used for bittering, spicy aroma, dry hopping.	Long, loose cones	High	Midseason
Eroica	This is one of the best varieties we grow because it is easy to care for, productive, and resistant to disease and insect damage. Bitter. Vigorous grower.	Large, tapered cones	High	Midseason
Fuggles	Traditional English ale hop. Prefers a wet climate and grows well in wet years. Used for both its mild aroma and bittering.	Small, round cones	Low	Early season
Galena	Very bitter, pungent U.S. hop bred from Brewer's Gold. High alpha acid content. Vigorous grower.	Medium, tight cones	High	Midseason
Goldings	A classic English ale hop bred from Fuggles. Starts slow, but grows more vigorously as season progresses. Susceptible to downy and powdery mildew.	Small, lightweight, fluffy cones	Moderate	Early to midseason
Hallertauer	U.S. version of traditional German lager hop. Likes cool, wet climates. Distinctive aroma.	Small, loose cones	Moderate	Early season

Variety	Characteristics	Cone Style	Yield	Ready for Harvest
Liberty	A U.S. hop with a spicy aroma.	Small, tight cones	Moderate	Midseason
Mt. Hood	Very aromatic hop; bred to resemble Hallertauer.	Compact, medium cones	Moderate	Midseason
Northern Brewer	Bold, bitter, aromatic German hop.	Medium, loose cones	Moderate	Midseason
Nugget	Fast-growing American bittering and aroma hop bred from Brewer's Gold. Highly disease resistant.	Long, dense cones	High	Midseason
Perle	German lager hop. Less vigorous than Eroica or Willamette, more productive than Fuggles. Lends a spicy taste and aroma similar to Hallertauer.	Long, tapered cones	Moderate	Early season
Saaz	Traditional Czech Pilsner aroma hop. Not very vigorous. Susceptible to downy mildew.	Small cones	Low	Early season
Spalt	German lager and ale hop with low bitterness, mild spicy flavor, and excellent aroma. Poor disease resistance.	Small, loose cones	Moderate	Early season
Target	English bittering and aroma hop. High alpha acid content. Tolerates wilt and resists powdery mildew, but susceptible to downy mildew. Somewhat difficult to train. Rare in North America.	Small, tight, plump cones	Moderate	Late season
Tettnang	Spicy, distinctive, popular German lager aroma hop. Tolerant of downy mildew.	Small, tight cones	Low	Early season
Willamette	American ale hop, bred to resemble Fuggles. Moderately bitter with a spicy aroma. Our favorite hop for home growing.	Large, tapered cones	High	Midseason

Siting the Hop Yard

The hop yard is the traditional name for any spot where hops are grown. Ideally, the hop yard should be a site with full sun and good air circulation. The number of hops you plan to grow will determine its size. Hops are usually grown in hills about 2½ to 3 feet (.8 to 1 m) apart, with one to two rhizomes per hill. For five plants you will need a bed 15 feet long by 3 feet wide (about 5 m X 1 m).

To insure an even, square bed you can lay out the area with stakes and strings beforehand. The hop bed can be located in the middle of the lawn if that's the best location you can find. If you're starting with lawn, cut and remove the sods with a spade. Make sure to get out all of the grass and weed roots. If you don't plan to plant right away, cover the bare soil with a layer of mulch to prevent weeds from taking hold. You'll need to mulch after planting, too; good, deep mulching is the secret to excellent hops.

IDEAL SITE CHECKLIST

Try to plant in an area with as many of the following characteristics as possible:

✓ Southern exposure for full sun — minimum of 6 to 8 hours of sun per day

✓ Good air circulation to help prevent diseases

✓ An existing wind break to prevent vine damage

✓ Plenty of vertical space — vines can reach heights of up to 30 feet

✓ Good drainage

✓ Accessible to water hose

✓ Existing structures that can be used for a trellis

Hop site measurements

Hops are usually grown in small hills about 6 to 7 inches (15 to 17 cm) tall and a few feet across. This helps to contain the roots and makes pruning both shoots and roots easier. Hop plants are pruned above and below ground; see page 23 for pruning vines and page 36 for root pruning.

Planting

Hops should be planted as early in spring as the soil can be worked, about the same time as early peas. For this reason you may want to consider digging the hop bed the autumn before you plan to plant. This is an especially good idea in areas with short growing seasons or where the soil takes a long time to dry out in spring. It's also a good idea if you're adding any amendments from the box on the next page, as all of these except sulfur need time to break down before plants can use them.

Soil Preparation

Soil in the hop yard should be a deep, heavy loam with good drainage. The vines are hardy enough to thrive in just about any kind of soil or conditions, but the yield will not be large on a poor soil.

Whenever it is prepared, the hop bed should be deeply spaded and improved with compost or well-rotted manure. If the soil of your hop yard is sandy, dry, and rocky, or even thick with chunks of clay, don't worry: The plants will grow in it. Amending the site with lots of organic matter such as compost or rotted manure and covering the area with a thick mulch of shredded leaves, straw, or hay will eventually result in a soil that's rich and friable enough for hops to thrive. Hops grow best in a soil that's not too acidic or alkaline, one with a pH range of 6 to 7.5. As a result, it's not a bad idea to use an inexpensive soil test to find out the pH level of your soil and what minerals may be lacking.

ADJUSTING SOIL pH

The pH scale used for measuring the acidity of garden soil is the same one used for homebrewing. Using certain amendments, you can raise or lower the pH of your soil to best suit the particular growing needs of your hops, brewing herbs, grains, and any other plant. Be warned that more is not better when it comes to soil amendments. Don't use more than the recommended amounts or you'll throw off your soil's nutrient balance.

Amendment	Effects	Rate of Application
Bonemeal	Raises pH. Excellent source of phosphorus.	3 pounds (1.3 kg) per 100 sq. feet (9 sq. m)
Compost	Slowly lowers pH of alkaline soils and raises pH of acidic soils. Supplies small quantities of many plant nutrients.	1 to 2 bushels per 100 sq. feet (9 sq. m)
Dolomite limestone	Raises pH. Adds lots of magnesium; if your soil doesn't need magnesium, substitute the same amount of calcitic limestone.	To raise pH about one point, add 7 pounds (3 kg) per 100 sq. feet (9 sq. m) on clay soil, 2 to 3 pounds (908 g to 1.3 kg) on sandy soil, 6 pounds (2.7 kg) on loamy soil
Phosphate, colloidal	Raises pH. Excellent source of phosphorus.	Up to 5 pounds (2.3 kg) per 100 sq. feet (9 sq. m)
Phosphate, hard rock	Slowly raises pH one point or more. Excellent, slow-release source of phosphorous; also supplies iron and other nutrients.	Up to 10 pounds (4.5 kg) per 100 sq. feet (9 sq. m)
Sulfur	Lowers pH of alkaline soil.	To lower pH about 1 point, add 1 pound (454 g) per 100 sq. feet (9 sq. m) on sandy soil, 1½ pounds (680 g) on loamy soil, 2 pounds (908 g) on clay soil
Wood ashes	Raises soil pH. Contributes potassium, magnesium, and other nutrients.	1 to 3 pounds (454 g to 1.3 kg) per 100 sq. feet (9 sq. m)

Hops are energetic plants and heavy feeders that require a lot of nutrients. They need nitrogen, phosphorus, potassium, magnesium, calcium, iron, zinc, boron, and molybdenum. Deficiencies of these will show themselves in dwarfing, small leaves, and poor color. Adding plenty of organic nourishment, such as compost or well-rotted cow manure, to the soil should take care of all of the plants' needs. Spread a 3-inch (about 8 cm) layer over each hill. We find that soil treated this way gets better and richer with time, unlike soils treated with chemicals (which need frequent re-stocking). Once the soil is enriched, you can form hills and plant.

TURNING SPENT BREWING GRAINS INTO RICH SOIL

You can reuse the waste leftover from your homebrewing to help your hop garden. It's as simple as finding an out-of-the-way spot on your property, dumping the spent grains, hops, and yeast from your latest batch, and letting it all rot. Composting does not have to be very scientific to work well. The key is exposing as much of the pile to good air circulation as possible. Anything from a bit of chicken wire wrapped around a few stakes to an elaborate wooden slat box can serve as a composter. In addition to your brewing waste, two basic types of materials go into a compost heap:
 ▶ moist greens — fresh cut weeds, vegetable scraps, etc.
 ▶ dry browns — leaves, dried weeds, dry grass clippings, etc.
Alternate between green and brown layers. Water each layer until just moist; water pile as needed to keep ingredients moist. Turn the pile every 4 weeks. Your grains and garden waste will eventually become moist rich compost your hops and other garden plants will love.

Planting the Rhizomes

Hop rhizomes should be planted horizontally, with the white shoots pointing up and the rootlets leading down and to the sides.

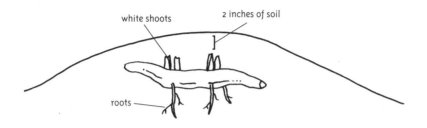

This illustration shows the proper rhizome planting position.

Dig a small trench about 6 inches (15 cm) deep in the top of the hill, place the rhizome in it, and cover it over with 2 inches (5 cm) of soil. The hop hills need to be spaced 2½ to 3 feet (80 cm to 1 m) apart, with one to two rhizomes per hill. We plant the same variety of hops together in the same hill to avoid future confusion. Then cover the hill with about a 1- to 2-inch (2.5 to 5 cm) layer of mulch, a loose blanket of organic material such as rotten straw. In between the hills, spread a thicker layer of mulch, 3 to 6 inches (8 to 15 cm) deep, to prevent weeds. Keep the ground around the newly planted hops moist with frequent, shallow waterings since the root systems will be small. The hills in the hop yard should always be kept evenly moist, without being saturated.

Don't remove the mulch as the plants start to grow; just leave it in place and the hop shoots will grow up through it. A layer of mulch keeps the ground from drying out around the plants, discourages pests and weeds, and reduces nitrogen loss from the soil. Add more mulch every so often throughout the season as the old mulch breaks down into the soil.

The Trellis

Hops can be grown up a wall; over a fence, stone wall or arbor; around a gazebo; or even up a flagpole. But for purposes of

KEEPING TRACK

It's important not to lose track of which plant is which, or you may be in for a surprise come brewing time. One way to do this is to make a map of your hop yard, noting which hop varieties are in which hills. Then put the map in a safe place. But because pieces of paper are very easy to lose, and for convenience during harvesting, you should also mark the hills. Your hops are going to be around for a long time, so you should use something very permanent. Plastic name tags tend to disintegrate or get lost after a few seasons. Metal stakes with the hop varieties engraved on them will last longer. These stakes can also double as an anchor for the trellis twine.

producing brewing hops that can easily be harvested, it is best to use a trellis, a sturdy structure designed to support vines. In commercial hop yards, vines are grown on 18-foot-tall (5.5 m) trellises with plants spaced 7 feet (about 2 m) apart.

When setting up the hop yard, the trellis may seem unnecessarily huge and intimidating. But you will be amazed how quickly your hops will cover it. Build the trellis properly the first time; this is a job you won't want to do again soon. Depending on where you site your hop yard, there may already be something nearby such as a building or a tree that you can use to support one or both ends of the trellis. In this case you can just screw in a set of hooks to support the top wire of your trellis, using a pair of turnbuckles to tension the wire. Otherwise, you'll have to install poles.

As an example of growing hops on the side of a house or outbuilding, a friend of ours plants his hills about 3 feet (1 m) apart along the sunny sides of his house and shop, with one plant per hill. He puts a tomato cage over each hill. Above each hill on the wall, at the highest point available, he puts a heavy screw eye. Then he ties two heavy twine strings to each bolt, and ties these off on either side of the cage. When the hop shoots appear, he trains three to each line and cuts back the rest. He grows all of his hops this way, and he grows a lot of hops.

Whatever kind of trellis you decide to build, it is vital that it be strong enough not only to support the weight of the masses of hop vines, but also to resist vine damage from high winds and storms. Adequate guying will help prevent this kind of damage. If your trellis is strong enough to support a ladder for harvesting, so much the better.

Tent Pole Trellis

Pole trellises come in several types. The single pole method, also called tent training, is very handy because you can train up to six hop plants on the guy lines. The pole can be made out of a 16-foot (4.8 m) piece of spruce, cedar, or locust wood. These woods are all readily available and none of them will rot. This will allow you to bury the base 3 feet (1 m) deep and still have 13 feet (4 m) of pole to work with. Another option is a metal pole of the same length, perhaps a section of aluminum irrigation pipe.

Prepare a hole for the trellis pole with a post-hole digger or shovel, digging down a little more than 3 feet (1 m). Put a large, flat stone in the bottom of the hole, center the pole, and backfill with gravel and small rocks to fill the hole. Check for plumbness with a carpenter's level. You can then guy the pole in three directions with $^3/_{16}$-inch galvanized wire to stakes or anchors about 7 feet (2.1 m) out from the pole. Put three galvanized ringbolts through the top of the pole to secure the guylines. Tie the guylines to the ringbolt and tape ends with waterproof tape. The other ends of the guylines may be tied directly to the stakes, once the stakes have been driven into the ground or you can attach them with turnbuckles to tension the lines.

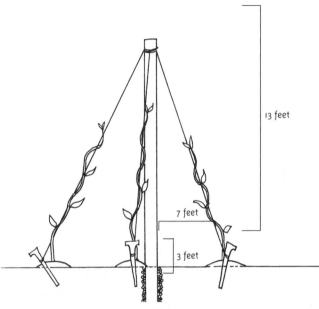

13 feet

7 feet

3 feet

Tent pole trellis system

Locate one hop hill just inside of each stake. The vines can easily be trained up the wires. Up to three additional hills can be located in the spaces between the first three. Some people who use tent trellises attach the hop lines to a sliding collar on the pole which can be raised and lowered with a rope and pulley. The advantage to this is that you don't have to climb up to harvest. Extra lines for these hop plants don't need to be so rugged; heavy twine will do.

Straight Pole Trellis

Another approach is to use a straight trellis of two or more poles in a series, guyed on either side and connected to each other by a top wire the length of your hop yard, or up to 25 feet (about 8 m). The straight pole trellis system is mainly used when you have plenty of room and want to set up your trellis like telephone poles. This system is much more common in European than U.S. hop yards.

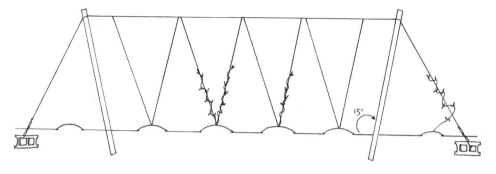

Straight pole trellis system

In commercial hop yards, the poles are angled away from each other at about 15 degrees. This gives a little extra strength to the trellis, as otherwise the poles tend to bow in toward each other under the weight of the adult hop plants. The wire passes through holes in the tops of the poles and is attached to buried anchors on either side of the trellis. A buried cinderblock makes a very strong anchor. If you drill holes and thread the wire through the poles before you raise them, you won't have to worry about how to get it up there later.

In our own hop yard, we've successfully used a trellis made of two heavy-duty, 2½-inch (6.3 cm) aluminum poles 13 feet (about 4 m) long spaced 20 feet (about 6 m) apart. To avoid the need for guylines, we sunk each pole 3 feet deep. The bases of the poles are set in cement. We bolted a 1-inch-diameter (2.5 cm) pole that was once part of a TV antenna between these as a crossbar. The result is a very solid trellis that will last us for years of hard use. It has no guylines to trip the unwary or to get tangled up with the lawnmower, and the storm that could blow it down would probably also take the house. Our trellis is only 10 feet (about 3 m) tall. This isn't as tall as some people recommend, but that makes it easier for us to reach the hop flowers at harvest. This size trellis is adequate for 2 to 3 mature hop vines.

Training the Vines

Hop vines can grow up to a foot a week; established plants can grow up to 30 feet (9 m) in a season. This vigorous growth needs to be checked so hops won't overwhelm your trellis, and also so that some of that prolific energy will be transferred to the production of hop cones.

When the young hop vine shoots start to appear early in the season; string twine in a v-shape between the top wire and small stakes or bent pieces of wire in each hop hill.

We use jute twine to train our hops. It's biodegradable, and when the hop vines die back we compost them, strings and all. Whatever type of twine you use, it works better if it's coarse — the texture will help the vine to hold onto the twine and climb more easily, reducing plant stress.

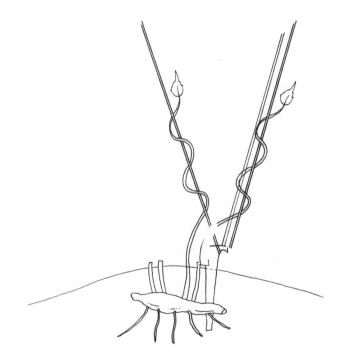

Training hop vines

Choose two or three of the healthiest looking vine shoots from each rhizome and prune off the rest. The remaining vines need to be trained up the tellis lines. The young vines should be wrapped around the lines in a clockwise direction (unless you live in the southern hemisphere; then train them counterclockwise). The growing tips at the ends of the vines are tough but brittle; be careful not to break them off. Try to train the vines on a warm, sunny day when they are the most pliable. The vines will only need encouragement for the first week or so; then they'll start climbing on their own. Once they reach the horizontal crossbar at the top of the trellis, they will have to be trained over it.

After selecting and training your main vines, prune off any new shoots that appear.

Watering

It is vital to keep your plants well watered during the growing season. Hops use a lot of moisture building those huge vines, and they need more to produce a bountiful harvest. On the other hand, watering too much will waterlog the roots and kill the plants. It's important to strike a balance. A good rule of thumb is that the hop hills should be evenly moist without being saturated. In dry weather and during cone production, new hop vines should be watered every day. You can use a sprinkler or a soaker hose, or just water by hand. Sprinklers should not be used in areas where the disease downy mildew is a problem, because dampness on the leaves will help the wind-borne mildew spores to germinate.

Hop Plant Nutrition

Hops grown in healthy, well-composted, nutrient-rich soil shouldn't suffer from nutrient deficencies. The best remedy for nutrient deficencies is to prevent them from happening in the

IDENTIFYING AND CORRECTING NUTRIENT DEFICIENCIES

Symptoms	Nutrient Deficiency	Deficiency Remedy
Light green leaves and stunted growth; leaves turn yellow before end of season; vines may turn a reddish color	Nitrogen	Add more compost and well-rotted manure to soil; give plants a quick boost with fish emulsion or blood meal.
Leaves are small, olive to orange colored, and curl under; spots appear on the veins; plants grow slowly	Phosphorus	Add colloidal phosphate or wood ashes to soil; give plants a quick boost with liquid seaweed.
Smaller than normal leaves with yellow edges; weak tip growth; leaves die and fall off	Calcium	Add limestone, wood ashes, or crushed oyster shells to soil.
Lower leaves turn bright yellow, then brown and die; condition spreads up the vine	Magnesium	Add dolomite limestone or langbeinite to soil, or spray plants with Epsom salts dissolved in water.
Tip growth turns yellow; youngest leaves turn yellow but veins remain green	Iron	Add colloidal phosphate or wood ashes to soil. Boost plants with a spray of liquid seaweed.
Leaves roll followed by bronzing and browning; leaves abnormally thin	Zinc	Add Azomite or wood ashes to soil and boost plants with a spray of liquid seaweed.
Earliest shoots abnormally thick before dying back; wrinkled leaves	Boron	Sprinkle each hill with $1/2$ teaspoon (2.5 ml) borax.
White speckling on leaves later turning to yellow; leaves curl upward	Molybdenum	Add Azomite or wood ashes to soil and boost plants with a spray of liquid seaweed.

first place by incorporating lots of compost or rotted manure before planting. This will insure that your soil contains an ample supply of nutrients for your hops. If you do encounter problems, use the chart on page 24 to help identify what's missing and add the appropriate soil amendments.

Hop Pests and Diseases

The best prevention against all kinds of insect and disease damage is to have healthy, well cared-for plants that get adequate moisture, sunlight, and food. Strong plants can fight off many pests and diseases that weak ones will not survive. Plants that are not overcrowded and that grow in nourishing soil will probably have

GROWING HOPS IN LIMITED SPACES

Just because you live in an apartment or some other place where growing space is very restricted doesn't mean you can't grow at least some of your own hops. If you have a porch that gets at least 6 to 8 hours of sunlight per day, consider growing a hop vine or two in 5-gallon (19 L) plastic buckets or larger containers. Train the vines along the porch railing or on lines strung from hooks along the edge of the roof. They'll need a very rich soil mix to start with, and more frequent watering than they would in the ground. Keep them well trimmed.

We can't guarantee huge yields using this method, but you will get enough hops to experiment with, and the plants will look great. Hops can stand very cold temperatures, but they should still be brought indoors to some cold spot to overwinter after they have died back. They will soon become rootbound in a pot; plan on dividing plants frequently.

Another limited space method is to locate some hop hills next to a south-facing porch overhang. You can grow two vines in each hill in a V-shape, with the twines tied to hooks screwed into the overhang. If you have a sturdy porch railing, you can stand on this to pick the hops. We've also heard of people mounting pulleys on second-story roof overhangs, with the hop twine leading through the pulleys. When the hops are ready to pick, the growers just lower the whole vine gently to the ground.

few problems to begin with; most of the ones that may arise can be handled organically without too much effort. Only in very persistent cases should you resort to an organic pesticide or fungicide. Consult your local garden center for the least toxic pesticide or fungicide that is appropriate for your particular problem, and be sure to follow all directions and precautions carefully.

Pests

Japanese beetle *(Popillia japonica)*

▸ **Description**

Oval-shaped, ½-inch-long (1.3 cm) beetles with gleaming, green bodies and bronze wing cases. They are found predominately in the eastern half of North America. In northern regions, the adults emerge in the late summer and remain active until frost.

Japanese beetle

▸ **Symptoms**

If you see huge holes in leaves and chewed cones, Japanese beetles are the culprit. They are the worst problem that we have experienced raising hops. Nothing else comes close. For some reason they love Fuggles and attack the plants voraciously.

▸ **Control**

The beetles are slow and stupid in the early mornings. It's easy to go out and flick them into jars of soapy water. You can also just grab the beetles off the leaves and crush them.

Locating the hop yard away from the beetles' favorite food plants such as roses, grapevines, and raspberry bushes will help. Beneficial nematodes (tiny soil organisms), are a good control. Dig them into the ground in the late spring or early summer when the soil is wet. They will destroy the overwintered grubs. This does nothing about the adult beetles that fly in from other areas, but it will prevent them from reproducing on your land.

Traps with sex lures are another control. They work by simulating the female beetle scent and attracting male beetles into a bag trap where they can't escape. These should be placed some distance upwind of the plants; otherwise they will draw more insects to your hops than they kill. Both beneficial nematodes and traps with sex lures can be purchased from many garden centers and mail-order catalogs, as well as from the sources in appendix B.

Spotted Cucumber Beetle

(Diabrotica undecimpuctata howardi)

Spotted cucumber beetle

▸ **Description**

The spotted cucumber beetle, sometimes called a squash beetle, is about ¼ inch (6 mm) long. It has a flat, oblong body with a yellow-green wing case. Twelve black spots on the body give this beetle its name. The adults lay eggs in the soil around the vines. Hatching larvae are beige colored and have a spot on their end body section. Both adults and larvae overwinter in the soil. They exist throughout North America, but they're more of a problem west of the Rocky Mountains.

▸ **Symptoms**

Cucumber beetles chew large holes with ragged, corky edges in leaves. Adults feed on stems and leaves causing damage to hop cones and the growing tips of the vines.

▸ **Control**

Adults can be captured by hand. Severe infestations can be controlled using botanical pesticides such as rotenone or pyrethrin, available from many garden centers and mail-order catalogs. Spray in the morning before the beetles become active. Cover the vines with an old bed sheet to prevent them from escaping the poison. Remember to allow at least two weeks to pass between spraying and harvest. Beneficial nematodes will control the larvae in the soil. If you had a bad problem the year before, consider relocating your hop yard, since the beetles ovewinter in the soil and will most likely return again. Straw mulch can help keep the beetles from traveling from plant to plant.

Hop aphid *(Phorodon humuli)*

▸ Description

These aphids are hop pests that damage hop vines in many areas throughout North America. They are tiny, only about $\frac{1}{10}$ inch (2.5 mm) long, and translucent green. They tend to feed in large colonies on soft, new growth.

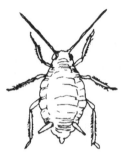

Hop aphid

▸ Symptoms

The aphids literally suck plants dry causing leaves to curl. They also spread aphid sooty mold, an unappetizing black fungus that grows on infected plants. They are usually found on the undersides of leaves, so turn over a few leaves to check for this pest.

▸ Control

If you get a major infestation of aphids, try blasting them with the hose every day for a week or so. Be sure to spray in the morning so the leaves can dry out before nightfall to avoid encouraging fungal diseases. Hop aphids can also be controlled by spraying leaves with a homemade soapy water mix (see box on page 30) or a store-bought insecticidal soap on the vines. Liberal applications of the light, powdery dust called diatomaceous earth directly on leaves and vines also work. It should be applied when the plants are wet, such as early morning or after a watering. The dust will dehydrate and eventually kill the insects. (The powder is very irritating to lungs and skin, so wear a dust mask and gloves.)

Japanese ladybugs *(Harmonia axyridis)* love to eat every aphid in sight. Introducing these beneficial insects to your hop yard should keep aphids under control. Purchased ladybugs are notorious for flying away before they've eaten many of your pests. (Native ladybugs are great and stick around.) If you want to buy predators, lacewings *(Chrysopa* spp.) are much better. They're voracious (also alled aphid lions), eating mites and some scale as well as aphids.

Spider mites *(Tetranychus urticae)*

▶ **Description**

Spider mites are tiny — only growing to a length of $\frac{1}{50}$ inch. You need a magnifying glass to see that they are a reddish to yellowish color and have eight legs. They are mainly a problem in hot, dry climates. Perversely, the mites also thrive when it's cold and wet. Unless plants are under some kind of water-related stress,

Spider mite

spider mites don't tend to attack them. They are most often found on the undersides of leaves. Mites can severely reduce your hop harvest or prevent it altogether.

▶ **Symptoms**

Spider mites suck plants dry in a similar way to aphids. Suspect them if leaves curl and become covered with tiny speckles. These pests also spin very small, fine webs where they are feeding, giving you a visual clue they are around.

▶ **Control**

Spray your homemade insecticidal soap mixture (see box on page 30) on the vines. They can also be controlled with diatomaceous earth in preference to chemical pesticides. Simply hosing down the vines regularly will control many infestations.

CLEAN UP PEST PROBLEMS WITH SOAP

Add 1 teaspoon (5 ml) of nondetergent soap to 1 quart (about 1 L) of water. This soapy mixture will kill soft-bodied pests like aphids and spider mites without hurting your hop plants. But just to be safe, test the mixture on a few leaves. Check for burning the next day — if the leaves look fine, spray the entire plant to kill off the insects.

Voracious lacewings (available from sources in appendix B) can help control spider mite populations. Mites have few other natural enemies, but new ones are now being developed by growers.

Diseases

You can prevent or minimize most diseases with a few simple tricks.

Morning waterings will allow the plants to dry out properly over the course of a day and not provide an easy, damp target for diseases. Spacing plants farther apart and thinning out leaves also helps by increasing air circulation, so leaves dry quickly. We suggest pruning off all leaves on the bottom 2 feet (60 cm) of the vine; do this when the plant reaches the top of your climbing twine.

Powdery Mildew

▶ Description

An outbreak of powdery mildew wiped out hop production in the eastern United States in the 1800s and the industry never recovered. More recently, professional growers in the Pacific Northwest have battled this fungal disease. It most often appears from July until the end of the growing season during periods of warm, humid weather with plenty of rainfall.

▶ **Symptoms**

Powdery mildew starts out as small, white spots on leaves and stems, spreading into a white powder that covers the entire leaf. The fungal spores can spread easily from leaf to leaf and plant to plant by the wind. The fungus will feed on the leaves and kill them.

▶ **Control**

Remove any infected leaves or stems immediately and burn them. Spray the vine and leaves with compost tea or manure tea (see box on page 32) in the morning every two weeks after the first sign of the disease. Baking soda spray (see box on page 34) is another good control. Wye Target and Nugget show some resistance to powdery mildew.

Downy mildew

▶ **Description**

This fungal disease is mainly a problem affecting western North American hop yards. The mildew loves cold, damp weather; as a result, it's more of a problem in northern regions than in the South.

▶ **Symptoms**

Look for the mildew in the early spring, when vine shoots begin to appear. Some shoots may develop into what are known as "basal spikes" that are obviously diseased: stunted, with sick-looking silver-and-black leaves. This mildew shows up on mature vines during the summer as a yellowing of the leaves that soon turns into a gray fuzz on leaf undersides. Infected plants may die if left untreated.

▶ **Control**

Remove and burn the diseased spikes as soon as they appear. Spraying with homemade compost or manure tea after first sign of the fungal disease with help as well.

Verticillium wilt and fusarium wilt

▸ **Description**

These two fungal diseases traditionally hit tomato plants and can sometimes affect hops. Our plants lose a few lower leaves to fusarium every season. Verticillium wilt has had a devastating effect on stocks of Hallertauer Mittelfrüh hops in Germany.

▸ **Symptoms**

Both diseases produce similar symptoms: The leaves turn yellow, developing corky brown patches that can spread to cover the whole surface. The leaves eventually wither and fall off. They can kill, but tend only to reduce cone harvests. Wye Target and Northern Brewer show some resistance.

▸ **Control**

Neither of these diseases can be cured, but both can be slowed down by spraying with a homemade baking soda solution or compost/manure tea. Fusarium can survive in soil for years without a suitable host; if it lives in your area you're probably stuck with it. Moving your hop yard to another location is one option. Both fusarium and verticillium overwinter on tomato debris, so if you compost your tomato plants, don't feed the compost to your hops. Similarly, don't spread infected hop vine debris on either hop or tomato beds.

COMPOST TEA AND MANURE TEA

Compost or manure tea is a great, inexpensive way of helping your plants fight off disease and feeding them at the same time. This mixture can be made up in any quantity you need. Add a shovelful of compost or manure to a bucket (2 shovelfuls for a 5-gallon [19 L] bucket) and fill with water. Stir the mixture and let it ferment for a few days. Strain out large chunks and add at least an equal amount of water, until it is the color of weak tea. Spray the tea onto your plants to control fungal diseases like powdery and downy mildew. Spray in the morning or late evening.

Harvesting

If you've done everything right, about midway through the season the vines will put out many short side branches covered with round, spiky looking buds, or *burrs*. These will eventually develop into hop cones. When the burrs appear, feed each hop hill with a few shovelfuls of compost or well-rotted manure. Also at this point, begin to water the vines every day to aid cone production. During cone formation, hops need more water, but overwatering is generally worse than underwatering. A few weeks after the burrs appear, the *bracts* and *bracteoles*, the petal-like structures of the hop cones, will start growing out of them.

It only takes a very short time between the appearance of the first bracts and the filling out of the hop cones. When the hop cones have fully developed, harvest time is right around the corner.

When to Harvest

In places where the growing season is long, you can expect several pickings from your hops, especially if you plant early and late varieties. The harvest season can be stretched out in some areas for several months, from June through September or even October. Short-season regions, such as New England, are generally confined to just one picking, with the earliest and latest plants bearing only weeks apart rather than months.

Hop cones should be picked at their peak of readiness, which means that you have to pay attention to how they are developing. The most obvious sign of readiness is the development of lupulin glands, small yellow grains clinging to the base of the bracts. A mature hop cone will be heavy with this yellow powder. When you begin to suspect that the hops are nearing maturity, pick a cone and pull or cut it open. The lupulin should be a dark yellow-gold, and there should be a strong hop aroma.

HOMEMADE BAKING SODA SPRAY

A good organic control for fungal diseases of all kinds, including verticillium and fusarium, is a homemade baking soda spray. Mix 1 tablespoon (15 ml) of baking soda (sodium bicarbonate) per gallon (3.8 L) of
water. It's very important to begin spraying the plants as soon as symptoms appear. Baking soda has a systemic effect on plants, helping them
to fight off the disease; it also kills the fungus organisms.

Mature cones feel different from green ones; they are somewhat lighter, and feel drier and more papery. They also give off an
aromatic resin that sticks to your hands when you are picking.

When past their prime for picking, hop cones will turn tan
along the edges of the bracts and then develop brown spots.
Finally, they turn brown and start to open. Don't use any hops
that have turned completely brown; even the tan and spotted
ones are not of the highest quality. If you have let them go this
long, it's best not to use them in beer.

How to Harvest

If you have a small hop yard, harvesting can be no more
complicated than pulling off the soft green cones and putting
them into paper or burlap bags. Use a ladder to reach the highest cones. Use both hands to gently detach the cones, spilling as
little of the lupulin as possible. It's a good idea to use a picking
bag that you don't have to hold on to; something that attaches to
your belt or goes over your shoulder like a newspaper carrier's
bag works well. We also wear light cotton gloves and a long-
sleeve shirt when harvesting to provide some protection against
the hop spines.

Our heavy-duty trellis is strong enough to lean a ladder
against, which makes it easy to reach the highest hops. Most
trellis designs are not this rugged, meaning that you'll need a tall

folding ladder or a specially built harvest ladder. If your trellis is short enough, you can use a stepladder to pick the hops.

The only alternative to a ladder is to cut down the plants and pick the hops off the ground. This means that you will only get one harvest, and such treatment can also damage the plants. Many commercial growers harvest their hops this way, since they are more concerned about large harvests than repeat pickings. But if you don't have to cut the plants at harvest time, you should avoid doing so and gain the advantage of repeat pickings. This way you can harvest only those cones that are at the peak of ripeness. Picking all the cones at once will get the harvest done more quickly, but it will also mean you have some unripe cones in your bag. Wait to cut vines until later in the season when the vines start to die back on their own.

Post-season Care

After frost has killed the green growth, cut back the vines level to the ground. Feed each hill with a few shovelfuls of compost or well-rotted manure and heap mulch over them. If your soil tends to be acidic, fall is the best time to add limestone or wood ashes. The vines can be chopped up and composted. If you want to make hop wreaths, you'll have to cut the vines while they are still fresh and pliable. The old brown growth is too brittle for wreaths; it will break before it bends.

PAST THEIR PRIME

Hops that are past their peak ripeness do not have to be thrown away. You can compost them, use them as animal feed, or stuff them into a small pillowcase for use as a "hop dream pillow." Traditionally, soporific qualities have been attributed to hops. Placing a small hop pillow inside one's pillowcase is supposed to help people sleep, but allergy sufferers should not try this.

EXPECTED YIELDS

In the first season, while the vines are getting established, you shouldn't anticipate more than a few ounces of hops per vine, though this can vary with the variety and growing conditions. The first year we planted hops we got a pretty good yield because it was a long, warm summer with good rainfall. Every year after that, we harvested twice as much as the year before. After the first year, you can expect anywhere from $\frac{1}{2}$ to 2 pounds (about 227 to 908 g) of hops per mature vine. How well you manage your vines will also contribute to how much yield is available. If you work with your vines — pruning, watering, and keeping on eye on their needs — you should get good yields.

Dividing and Root-pruning Plants

Hop plants should be divided, or at least severely root-pruned, every three years. In an established hop yard, an annual spring root pruning is also a good idea. Rhizomes should be pruned before the new shoots are 6 inches (15 cm) tall. Use a clean, sharp knife to make neat cuts. Unlike many other plants, hops aren't fussy about how they're pruned. The rhizomes will grow back more prolifically than before. Cut back the roots to a 1-foot (30 cm) square around the crown. Pull up the outer roots and dispose of them. Make sure not to leave any severed root pieces in the ground, or they will continue to grow.

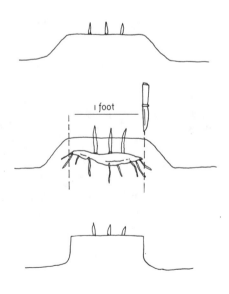

You can also divide off rhizomes from your hop plants. This should be done as soon as plants show any growth in spring. Again, use a clean, sharp knife, and cut the rhizome into several pieces, each with some sprouts and roots. If you're ambitious you can use the rhizomes to start another hop yard, or give them away to home-brewing friends. Incidently, this is a good way to get rootstock if you know someone who grows hops. Just show up and offer to help on pruning day and you'll get more roots than you can use.

Drying Hops

Drying should be done as quickly as possible after the harvest to preserve the essential hop oils. Warmth, no sunlight, and good air circulation are all that's required. Under very humid conditions, hops will take longer to dry. Once the hops are picked, they should never again be placed in direct sunlight, or even strong artificial light. Light-struck hops will add skunky off-flavors to beer.

Air Drying

Small harvests can be air-dried. Just place the hops in paper bags and leave them in a warm, dry place with good air circulation, such as an attic. Shake the bags every few days to aerate them. This method can also be used with larger harvests; just remember to use a lot of bags and put a small amount of hops in each one. If you have too many hops in one bag, they won't dry well and may spoil. This method should take a few days to one week depending on how humid the weather is.

IS THE HOP DRY?

A thoroughly dry hop feels light and dry to the touch, and a little springy. The cones will open slightly, and the lupulin will drop out if the cone is dropped from any height or tapped with a finger. If you strip all the bracts off, the remaining stem (called a *strig*) will almost break before it bends.

AVOID OVENS

It may seem obvious to use the oven on its lowest setting to dry hops. Don't try it; it drives off the hops' delicate volatile oils and renders them unfit for brewing. Not only that, it will fill your house with an unbeliev-ably strong and lasting odor of hops. Using a food dehydrator will also produce a strong hop smell and will blow lupulin into the air, which could cause problems for the allergy sufferers in your household. Neither of these difficulties arises with air drying.

We also know of homebrewers who have air-dried their hops on old window screens. This method also takes up to one week. It's important to keep the screens in a dark, dry place with good air circulation. If dust is a problem, the hops should be covered with cheesecloth.

Dehydrators

Commercially available food dehydrators such as the American Harvest Snackmaster and Excalibur 2500 work well for hops. They have the added advantage of allowing you to control the temperature. We have found that 95°F (35°C), the lowest possible setting, works well enough and doesn't damage the hops. The only real problem with food dehydrators is that they don't hold very many hops at once, and they may take as long as 36 hours to dry the harvest.

The Oast

For large harvests, ones measured in pounds rather than in ounces, you will need a hop dryer, or *oast*. The standard oast is a box holding two or more drawers with screen bottoms and a hot-air system for drying the hops. An oast allows you to dry hops rapidly under controlled conditions. It is very handy for large crops. One oast can serve several growers since you won't be using it all the time.

Making an Oast

We have designed a modular oast that uses bins rather than drawers. It looks something like a beehive. This system is simple and inexpensive to build and very rugged. It allows you to use any number of bins, from one for small harvests to three or four for large ones. To build a simple two-bin oast, you will need:

Two 8-foot (2.4 m), 1 x 6 inch softwood boards
One 8-foot (2.4 m), 2 x 4 inch softwood board
One sheet ½-inch plywood, finished on both sides
36 galvanized 2-inch screws
24 galvanized 1½-inch screws
Two 25 x 25 inch (63.5 x 63.5 cm) square sheets of galvanized or bronze ¼-inch mesh screen
½ pound 2-inch galvanized nails
1 hair dryer, preferably the old fashioned hose-and-balloon type

1. To make the bins, cut each 1 X 6 into four 24-inch sections. The boards are then butt-jointed (fastened end-to-end without overlap) together with wood glue and 2-inch screws to form two boxes, each 25 inches on a side and 6 inches high. Use three screws per joint.

2. Make the base the same way as the bins, using the 2 X 4. Drill three ½-inch holes in each side of the base to allow free airflow during drying.

3. Invert the bins and lay the screens across the bottoms. Cut eight 1 X 24-inch plywood strips. Place the plywood strips along the edges of each frame, on top of the screen. Nail them to each 1 X 6 so that they hold the screens securely in place and protect their edges.

4. Cut two 25 X 25 inch square plywood pieces. Set aside one of these to use as the oast top. Use glue and nails to attach the other to the bottom of the oast base.

5. Cut out twelve 5 X 3 inch clamps from the remaining plywood. Fasten these to the top edges of the bins and base with glue and 1½ inch screws as shown in the plan. These serve to hold the bins together, and hold the top and base to the bins.

6. To finish the oast top, cut a hole in the center exactly the size of end of the hair dryer hose.

All wood used in your oast should be clean and untreated. After completion, the oast should not be painted, stained, or varnished. We recommend using galvanized metal fasteners and screens because drying hops give off a lot of moisture and this can cause rusting.

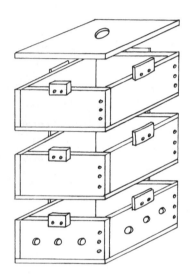

Using the Oast

It's not a bad idea to dry your hops outside, because the dryer could conceivably overheat and cause a fire. In our experience, this is more likely to happen with modern hand-held hair dryers than older types that use hoses. These older machines also usually have a greater number of heat settings, allowing you to finely control the drying temperature.

Fill the bins *loosely* (up to about ½ inch fom the top) with hops, and stack them on top of the base. Then cover the uppermost bin with the oast top. Press down on top of the oast to seat everything firmly. If any gaps show, you may want to place some small weights such as bricks on top of the oast to help press everything together. Then fit the hair dryer into the oast top and turn it on, set to low heat.

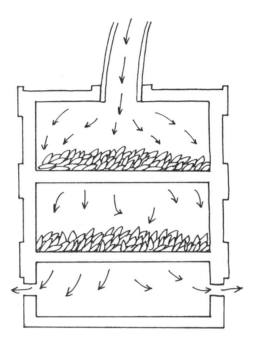

Fill the bins loosely so that air can circulate through the lower bins.

The hair dryer will provide enough heat and air circulation to dry several pounds of hops in 24 hours. The drying temperature inside your oast should be 110 to 160°F (43 to 71°C). You can take the temperature with a thermometer through the ½-inch holes in oast base. The upper bin or bins will dry first, so you can remove it and bag the hops while the bottom bin is drying.

Hop Storage

Once your hops are completely dry, they should be sealed in freezer bags with as much air as possible squeezed out. If you plan to use the hops right away, you can place them in the refrigerator. Otherwise, freeze all bags. Make sure to write the hop type and date on each bag with a magic marker. You might also

---

HOP TIP

A standard 1-gallon, zip-seal freezer bag stuffed full of hops weighs about 1 ounce (28 g). This is handy when it comes to using them in homebrewing; half a bag equals ½ ounce (14 g), and two bags equals 2 ounces (57 g).

---

want to keep an inventory of your hops in a notebook so you'll know what's available when developing recipes. We've kept hops in a freezer for upwards of a year with no loss of quality.

A large free-standing freezer is ideal for storing hops. If you plan to keep anything else in there, it's probably a good idea to put the hops in cardboard boxes. Otherwise, they can get crushed or drift around the freezer as you move things.

Since dry hops are very light and bulky, a freezer bag won't hold too many, even though they will compress almost indefinitely. We've found that stuffing a bag with hops and then crushing it down while zipping the bag shut at the same time is a good method. Hops don't keep when exposed to air, so exclude as much air from the storage bags as possible.

Using Homegrown Hops

Homegrown hops can have different characteristics than store-bought hops, so you may need to adjust your old recipes depending on your crop. Otherwise, you can use them in any beer recipe just like any other kind of hop. Better yet, you can design your own recipes around the particular characteristics of your own hops. In chapter 4, most of the recipes have been formulated with the use of homegrown hops in mind.

When you go to the homebrew store to purchase ingredients, remember that you have your own hops to use. It's easy to forget and automatically buy hops when putting together a recipe. By keeping in mind what varieties and what quantities you have, you can plan your brewing to fit your hop inventory.

Using as Finishing Hops

The aroma and flavor of fresh homegrown hops can't be surpassed. There's little point in boiling them away just to bitter your beer. In your first season, the harvest will probably not be large, so you can use this opportunity to try out your homegrown hops for dry hopping or as late-boil flavoring or aroma hops. Beer styles such as bitter, extra special bitter, pale ale, India Pale Ale, and California common beer that express a strong hop character are improved tremendously by the use of homegrown hops.

Using as Bittering Hops

We still buy most of our own bittering hops from the homebrew store, but once in a while we supplement store-bought bittering hops with fresh ones. As alpha acid percentages for the same variety vary greatly between years and places, it's difficult to tell exactly how bitter a particular batch of hops will be before you brew with it. This is one of the challenges that makes the use of homegrown hops for bittering a bit of a gamble.

In the commercial hop arena, each batch is rigorously tested for bitterness and graded accordingly. Serious homebrewers can also have their own hops graded scientfically in a similar way for bitterness. Some laboratories in hop-producing areas, such as Murphey Labs in Yakima, Washington, will conduct alpha and beta acid tests on your seasonal samples for a fee. Remember, though, that the results will be only for that year's crop and that alpha acid percentages fluctuate from year to year.

There is also a complex test you can do yourself known as the taste-titration method. Essentially it has to do with taste-testing the bitterness of a batch of beer brewed with your hops against a beer of known IBU *(International Bitterness Units)*. A complete description of this test is too lengthy to include here; one can be found in Mark Garetz's book, *Using Hops* (HopTech, 1994). This is really only important if you plan to enter your beer in a contest.

A simpler approach, if you want to use your own hops for bittering and aren't interested in the chemical niceties, is just to take the plunge! If you have taken reasonable care with your plants, picked the hops on time, and dried them carefully, your hops are probably perfectly fine for bittering. It will just take a little experimentation to discover exactly how to use them. Measure out your bittering hops carefully by weight and make, let us say, a simple batch of extract bitter. When you sample the beer, your own tastebuds will tell you if you got the amounts right. After you've brewed a few batches of beer using your own bittering hops (and kept careful records of your brewing procedure and beer taste), you should have a pretty good idea of how best to use your own hops.

You could also try a side-by-side brewing test. Brew two identical batches of beer, using store-bought whole hops in one batch and an equal amount of your own hops of the same variety in the other. Judicious tasting, preferably with some friends around to help out, should tell you a lot about the strength, bitterness, and quality of your hops.

Another easy solution to estimating hop bitterness comes from a friend and fellow homebrewer who uses his own hops often for bittering. He assumes his hops are the freshest and strongest available, and then uses the commercial specification for the hop variety he is using as a guideline. He always adds a little less of his hops than is called for in recipes to account for the homegrown freshness factor. He says he has yet to overbitter any of his beers using this simple method.

Brewing Herbs

*Our English Mum-makers use Sassafras and Ginger, the Rind
of Walnut Tree, Elecampane Root, Water Cresses, and Horse
Radish root rasp'd, Betony, Burnet, Marjoram, Mother of Thyme,
Pennyroyal of each a small handful, of Blessed Thistle a handful,
of Barberries bruised half an ounce, of Cardamums bruised
an ounce and a half. All of these are to be put in when the
liquor has wrought a while. . . .*

— The Receipt Book of John Nott, 1723

TODAY hops are the primary brewing herbs, but this was not always true. Throughout history hop cones were just one of many different kinds of herbs used to flavor and preserve beer. Hops came to prominence because they are so adaptable: They can be used for bittering, flavoring, or aroma, depending on when they are added to the boil. They also help preserve the finished beer.

Though hop use in brewing began thousands of years ago, hops were not used in European beers until the time of Charlemagne (about 800 A.D.) and did not appear in English beers until 1300. The term "ale," in fact, used to refer only to unhopped beer.

Hops were even occasionally banned as a brewing ingredient in some countries during the fifteenth and sixteenth centuries. England's notorious King Henry VIII outlawed hops to protect the income he gained from more lucrative brewing ingredients such as spices and other herbs.

Even without laws, the English preferred their traditional bittering herbs — and the more the better. Old recipes, like the one quoted for Mumm (a dark herbal ale), could include a couple of dozen different herbs and spices. Often these were added in the form of an "ale grout" made of a mixture of herbs such as burnet, betony, wild thyme, marjoram, elder flowers, rosemary, sage, chamomile, and mint. Usually herbs were added to the cask after the fermentation died down, just as dry hops are today. Sometimes herbs were steeped in the beer just before drinking.

Herbal beer is an old art that is being rediscovered by many brewers, though it hasn't been that long since herbal beers were common and popular. According to Michael Jackson's *Beer Companion* (Running Press, 1993), many large British breweries stopped using ginger and licorice in ale as little as 40 years ago. The Belgians have never given up the use of herbs as key ingredients for their storied beers, a regional tradition that goes back hundreds of years.

There are of course alternatives to growing all your own brewing herbs. Many of the more common herbs are available in fresh or dried form either in the supermarket, homebrew store, or health food store. But some herbs are more difficult to find; for some of these, about the only approach is to acquire some seeds and grow the plants. Dried and fresh herbs have different characteristics, and it's nice to be able to use both in brewing. And there is no question that your own homegrown herbs, even if used dried, will be better, fresher, and more aromatic than any you can buy.

Using Brewing Herbs

Brewing herbs have different characteristics, just as different hop varieties do. Most herbs traditionally associated with brewing are bitter. Others are more flavorful or more aromatic. What you use an herb for and when you use it depend on the qualities of the herb and the kind of beer you wish to brew. Some herbs are multipurpose, though none approaches hops in overall utility. Beer without any hop character at all is an acquired taste. We usually add at least ½ ounce (14 g) of hops for a 5-gallon (19 L) batch of even our most herbal beers.

Bittering Herbs

Bitter herbs include horehound, sage, dandelion, alecost, milk thistle, nettle, yarrow, gentian, clary sage, and betony. Add these at the beginning of the boil in place of or in addition to bittering hops. The bitterness that they add to beer will not necessarily resemble hop bitterness, and some may add medicinal or other unusual flavors. So it's best to go easy at first.

USING DRY VS. FRESH HERBS

When following recipes, always use half as much dried herbs as fresh. Roots are the exception; they must always be dried before they are used in brewing.

Flavoring Herbs

Herbs that can be used for flavoring include juniper, spruce, rosemary, hyssop, borage, ginger, oregano, mints, bee balm, lemon balm, sweet woodruff, marjoram, elecampane, licorice, and thyme. Most of these are strong-flavored; unlike aromatic hops, they should be added near the beginning of the boil. The more delicate ones like borage and lemon balm can be added to the last 15 minutes of the boil. Some of the flavoring herbs also have powerful aromas; these do double duty when added to beer.

Aromatic Herbs

Rosemary, hyssop, lavender, chamomile, lemon balm, bee balm, elder flowers, and many other herbs can be used to

STEEPING HERBS

Steeping herbs in a small amount of vodka prior to using them as a brewing ingredient can allow you to make the herbal essences more distinct. This method is used mainly for adding flavor and aroma. Sufficient bitterness can be expressed in the boil. Using this method with bitter herbs such as horehound might produce excessive bitterness. This step also lets you test whether or not you like the herb before adding it to your brew. Place the herbs you want to use in a large, clean glass jar. Use slightly more herbs than you expect to need in your batch. Pour in enough of an inexpensive brand of vodka to cover the herbs. There should be about twice as much vodka as herbs by volume in the jar. Seal the jar and let it steep for a week, shaking it occassionally. Taste the potion and add more herbs if needed. Steep for another week and strain. Add the mixture to the beer at bottling time or during secondary fermentation. More scentific homebrewers can determine exactly how much of this potion to add with the following formula: Use a measuring pipette calibrated in tenths of a milliliter and a 1-ounce (28 g) sample of your beer to determine the ratio of potion to beer that you desire (in tenths of a milliliter per ounce). One ounce x 128 (ounces per gallon) x 5 (gallons per batch) = 640. Multiply R (amount of potion added to 1 ounce of beer) x 640 to get the amount of potion to add in milliliters to a batch to make it taste like your 1-ounce sample.

provide aroma to beer. Just drop the dried herbs into the last few minutes of the boil as you would with aroma hops.

Any of the aromatic herbs can also be used for dry hopping. Rosemary, a wonderfully aromatic herb, is a good choice for dry hopping. A few sprigs dropped into the carboy for a few days to a week before bottling will add a delicate, piney nose to the beer. Elderflower makes a good dry-hopping herb for mead making as well as beer brewing. Loose, dry herbs can be bagged in a hop bag for dry hopping so they won't get all through the beer. Don't worry about infecting your brew with dry herbs; the microorganisms that live on herbs can't survive in the acidic, alcoholic environment of finished beer.

Herb Cultivation

Herbs aren't very difficult to grow, though for some reason many people think the opposite is true. Most herbs are easy to cultivate and propagate either indoors or outside. Many are hardy and weedlike; once established some are so invasive that they can become a nuisance in your garden. This is especially true of mint-family herbs such as oregano. For this reason, it's usually a good idea to establish a separate herb bed, at least for invasive herbs. A few herbs can tolerate some shade, but most require full sun. Your bed should be in a sunny location with good air circulation and a slightly acidic to slightly alkaline, moderately loamy soil.

Because they tend to contain pungent oils and have strong aromas, herbs are less susceptible to insect damage than most other plants. Even if they are attacked, there will probably be an ample supply left for brewing purposes. Never spray your herbs with any kind of pesticide. A blast of water from the hose or soapy water should control the rare pest.

Herb Propagation

Growing Herbs from Seeds

Unless you already have full-grown plants to divide, seeds are usually the surest and easiest way to propagate plants. When you get your seeds, generally the packets will be labeled with growing instructions. If not, look for information in the seed catalog that you ordered from. At the very least, it should tell you if the seeds should be planted indoors or outdoors, and the number of weeks before the frost-free date that they should be planted. Some seeds require cold to germinate; just put the unopened packet in the refrigerator for 6 to 8 weeks before sowing.

Sow the seeds in a sterile seed-starting or potting soil mix. Never use garden soil or soil mixes that don't say "sterile" on

SANITIZING CONTAINERS

If you're reusing old planting containers, first wash them thoroughly in hot, soapy water. You may even want to sanitize them with a weak (10 percent) bleach solution, for much the same reason as you do in brewing. Bad microorganisms can get in there and spoil all the fun.

the label; they tend to harbor the spores of damping-off disease, which can kill an entire flat of seedlings in a matter of days.

Plant large seeds ¼ inch (6 mm) deep. Very small seeds should be just barely covered with soil mix. A rule of thumb is that seeds should be planted to a depth that is 3 times their length. Most germination failures are caused by planting too deep. Label your planted containers with the name of the plant and the date, so that you can tell at a glance which plants are which, and when you planted. Water well.

Cover the containers with plastic wrap and move them to a warm place out of direct light until the seeds sprout. Sometimes this germination takes up to two weeks. During this process, keep the soil medium damp. When the seeds sprout, move them either onto a sunny windowsill or under a growlight. As the plants grow, pot them up to bigger containers. The plants should have enough space so that their leaves don't touch. Don't let the soil dry out.

When the frost-free date has passed and the weather begins to settle, start hardening off the plants to prepare them for outdoor life. Hardening off means moving plants outside into the sunlight for an increasing number of hours per day for a week or so. Start with only a couple hours to keep sunlight from burning the tender leaves. Begin to decrease your watering. After the plants have hardened off for at least a week and have spent one night outside, they are safe to transplant into the garden. Hardening off is a necessary step; without it, the plants will die of transplant shock.

Some of the hardier herbs can be sown directly outside. Plant them outside either on the frost-free date or when the packet indicates. Keep them well watered until they sprout. Once they sprout, thin them to the distance recommended on the seed packet.

Growing Herbs from Divisions

As perennial plants grow, they often form large clumps and then begin to slow their growth. Division is a means of both making new plants and rejuvenating old ones.

Before you divide a plant, consider its growth habit. Does it form a tough, woody clump, like yarrow or bee balm? Or a loose crown, like betony or sweet woodruff? Perhaps it sprawls, sending out runners in all directions like thyme or oregano. The way the plant grows will determine how you'll divide it.

Plants should be dug up carefully before dividing. Push a garden fork or shovel into the ground all around the plant, rocking gently back and forth until the clump is loose. Then lift out the clump, trying not to injure the roots.

Woody-rooted plants can be split, either with two forks back-to-back or with a shovel. Each division should be at least 4 inches across (10 cm). Loose-crowned clumps should be pulled apart carefully by hand into individual plants, discarding any that look unhealthy or have few roots. To divide runner-forming plants, just cut off the runners at the base with a knife. Each runner can be replanted separately, but you'll get bigger plants faster by planting several runners at each new site.

All new divisions should be replanted and watered in as soon as possible. Dig a planting hole for the new divisions deep and wide enough to fit all roots; spread a thin layer of compost at the bottom. Water thoroughly to settle soil around roots. Keep watering until plants are established in their new locations, about six weeks. Divisions can be made either in the spring or fall. But if you divide in fall, bear in mind that the plants should be well established by the time the ground freezes.

Growing Herbs from Softwood Cuttings

Many perennials can be propagated by taking softwood cuttings. The best time to do this is late spring or early summer. Select 3- to 5-inch (8 to 13 cm) branches from the current year's growth that don't have flowering buds. Cut them off carefully with a clean, sharp knife or razor blade. Cut slightly below where a leaf stalk joins the stem. Remove the lower leaves (step A in illustration).

Fill a pot with damp sand or sterile soil mix. Make a hole in the soil for each cutting with a pencil. Plant the cuttings in the holes, making sure the end of the cutting is in contact with the soil (step B in illustration). Gently firm soil around cuttings. Seal the whole pot in a plastic bag and place it out of direct light. Check the pot periodically to make sure it doesn't dry out. In two weeks, gently pull on a cutting to see if roots are developing. If not, pull it out and check for rot. If it seems all right, put it back. When the cuttings develop roots, transplant them into individual pots.

Growing Herbs from Root Cuttings

Plants with thick, fibrous roots such as ginger, ginseng, elecampane, licorice, elder, and horehound can be successfully propagated from root cuttings. Carefully dig up the plant while it's dormant (generally early spring or late fall). Wash the soil off the roots. Select roots as thick as a pencil and cut them off close to the crown with a clean knife. Replant the mother plant immediately, and water it well.

Cut the roots into 2- to 4-inch (5 to 10 cm) lengths. To tell top from bottom, mark them with angled cuts. Cut the top end flat across and make a slanting cut on the bottom end. Fill a pot with damp sand or sterile soil mix. Make a hole in the soil for each cutting. Plant each one with the flat end flush to the soil surface and the slanted end down. Cover the soil with a light layer of crushed gravel, available at a garden center or pet store,

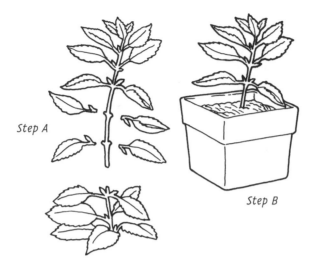

Step A

Step B

Propagating an herb from a softwood cutting

and place them inside on a window sill or outside in a cold frame until the cuttings root. When the cuttings show top growth, pot them up to individual pots.

Growing Herbs from Hardwood Cuttings

Some plants, such as alecost, can be propagated by hardwood cuttings taken in the late fall or early winter. Select a healthy, woody branch of the current year's growth. Cut just above a bud. Remove any side shoots and cut the branch into 3- to 5-inch (8 to 13 cm) pieces. Make an angled cut just above a bud, and a straight cut at the base. With a clean, sharp knife

SMALL-SPACE HERB GARDENING

Most herbs take easily to containers. Some warm-climate perennials require containers as they must be moved indoors in the fall to overwinter. Planting herb seeds in a pot is no different from planting them in the ground, except that you can do it at any time of the year. Container herbs can thrive just as much as those planted in the ground if proper care is taken with watering, sunlight, and dividing roots when needed.

or razor blade, cut away some of the outer bark near the base to expose the green, living layer (called the cambium) just underneath.

Plant the cuttings in individual pots of gritty soil mix (a half-and-half combination of sterile soil and coarse sand or perlite). Water them well and place inside on a windowsill or outside in a cold frame until they root. Hardwood cuttings take longer to root than other types; they should root by midspring of the following year. When the cuttings show top growth, transplant them into larger pots.

Growing Herbs from Offshoots

Plants like Roman chamomile can be propagated from basal offshoots. These are small, leafy shoots that cluster around the base of the mother plant, or the first growth that appears in early spring. When the shoots are $1\frac{1}{2}$ to 2 inches (3.8 to 5 cm) high, cut them off as close to the base as possible with a sharp knife.

Trim the stem ends of the offshoots, making a straight cut, and plant them in a pot filled with damp, sterile soil mix. Seal the pot in a plastic bag to conserve moisture. Be sure the soil remains moist but not wet and remove any dead or dying foliage to prevent rot. The offshoots should be well rooted within a month. Separate them and transplant them into their own pots.

Seasonal Care

Once herbs have become established, most varieties require little routine care. For perennial herbs, maintainence consists of occasional watering, weeding, mulching, and then cutting back the plant after it dies down in the fall. Herbs that are primarily grown for their leaves may be pinched or cut back frequently to encourage a steady supply of new growth. Invasive herbs such as those in the mint family should be watched carefully and cut back vigorously if they try to escape their beds. Cut off all faded blooms on herb plants (this is called "deadheading") to encourage reblooming and to prevent plants from forming seeds and self-sowing. (If you want new seedlings popping up in your garden, let a few flowers ripen into seeds.) Keeping herbs well mulched during the season protects leaves from getting dirty; mulch also holds in moisture and slowly feeds the soil.

Harvesting

The best time to harvest herbs is in the morning of a dry, sunny day after the dew has dried. Morning is the best time to harvest because the herb's essential oils are at their peak. A dry, sunny day ensures that the herbs won't have any excess moisture on them, which can cause problems such as spotting and mildew during drying. Leaf herbs such as oregano, thyme, and mints should be harvested just before the plants bloom, in late spring or early summer. If you begin harvesting herbs for drying early in the season, you can harvest more than once. As much as three-quarters of the season's growth can be cut at a time, unless

WILD GATHERING

Many brewing herbs can be gathered from the wild. Over time varieties that were originally cultivated have gone wild and now flourish in forests, fields, and waste spaces. Some candidates for gathering from the wild are dandelions, juniper berries, blackberries, wintergreen leaves and berries, wild apples and crabapples, wild hops, rose hips, blueberries, cranberries, nettles, milk thistle, elder flowers and berries, birch tips, yarrow, spruce boughs for spruce beer, and apple boughs and hickory bark for smoking grains. Please note that you should only gather wild plants from areas where they are plentiful, and you must ask for permission first before collecting plants on someone else's property.

If you live along the coasts, you can even gather shaggy brown bunches of Irish moss (seamoss) to dry and use as a fining agent in beer. Make sure to wash it thoroughly before air-drying to remove any sand particles. Once dry, Irish moss can be stored indefinitely in plastic bags.

CLEANING HERBS

Leaf and flower herbs should be reasonably clean when they come in from the garden. Carefully brush off any obvious dirt with a clean, dry paintbrush. If herbs are really dirty, gently rinse them with a watering can an hour or two before you intend to harvest. Roots, such as elecampane, should be thoroughly rinsed with water and dried with a towel.

otherwise indicated in the plant description. Always harvest herbs with a knife or sharp scissors; otherwise you may uproot the plants.

If you're harvesting leaves, always cut stems; they are much easier to dry, especially if you're hanging them. If you're using fresh herbs, cut them just before you brew, to preserve as much herb flavor as possible. Soft, delicate herbs like basil really should be used as soon as possible after picking; they can begin to brown in a few hours. Woody herbs like hyssop and rosemary can keep in the refrigerator for up to one week.

Most leaf herbs can be harvested throughout the season. Harvest annual herbs before frost kills them. Just pull annuals up by the roots late in the season. Perennials should only be cut up to a month before the first frost; otherwise they will be weakened going into winter. To be safe, plan your final harvest of perennial herbs six weeks before you expect frost. Flowers usually only appear for a short time; cut them before they are fully open, since they will continue to open as they dry. Seeds should be harvested before they begin to fall from the seedheads. Root crops are generally harvested in late summer or fall.

Drying Methods for Herbs

Herbs, like hops, can be dried in commercial food dehydrators on the lowest setting. But there are many alternatives if you don't own a dehydrator.

Air Drying

If your harvest is small, you can rack-dry it in a well-ventilated room out of direct sunlight. Use a screen, bamboo tray, or cheesecloth-covered cookie sheet. Lay the herbs in a single layer so they don't overlap. Turn or stir the herbs once a day until they dry. If dust is a problem, cover them with another sheet of cheesecloth.

For larger crops, there are several effective ways of drying herbs. To air-dry herbs, gather them in small bunches; large bunches will rot in the center. Tie the bunches tightly with string or elastic bands and hang them upside down in a warm, dark, dust-free environment for about two weeks until they dry. To protect them from dust and light and catch falling herbs, cover the herbs with a paper bag and tie the opening around the stems. Another method is to dry herbs using the oast described in chapter 1.

Conventional Oven Drying

Although it should be avoided with hops, oven drying is another possibility for some herbs. With a gas oven, leave the pilot light on and spread the herbs in a single layer on a cookie sheet. Leave the oven door ajar to allow air circulation. Turn the herbs once a day; they should dry in one to three days. With an electric oven, turn it to the lowest setting for a few hours. Conventional ovens are generally too hot for leaf herbs which should be dried at 90 to 110°F. Roots can be safely oven-dried.

DRYING ROOT HERBS

Roots such as licorice, gentian, and elecampane can be dried using a food dehydrator, oven, or microwave. Chop them first for faster drying. Store them in sealed glass jars away from light and heat.

Microwave Oven Drying

Even the microwave oven can be used to dry herbs. Choose a dry day to work; humid weather can prevent herbs from drying properly. Brush any soil from the leaves and stems with a clean, stiff paintbrush. Place about a cupful in the microwave between paper towels and microwave on high for 1 minute. Delicate herbs like marjoram should be turned every 30 seconds. If they aren't dry yet, microwave again for 20 seconds. Remember that foods cooked in the microwave tend to continue cooking for a while after they come out. Drying time will depend on the moisture in the herbs, the humidity in the air, and the power of your microwave. It may require some experimentation to get it right. It's better to let still-moist microwaved herbs air dry for a while than to burn them. A method that works as well or better is to hang freshly picked herbs to air-dry for a few days before finishing them in the microwave.

Refrigerator Drying

Herbs like rosemary and hyssop, which are not as delicate as other herbs, may be dried in the refrigerator. Put a few sprigs in a paper bag in the refrigerator for about a month. They will be green, springy, and feel dry to the touch.

Storage

When the leaves are fully dry, strip them off the stems. Store them either in dark glass bottles in a cool place out of the direct sun, or in zip-seal bags in the freezer as for hops. Don't store dried herbs on a rack above the stove; the steam and heat from cooking will cause their flavors to deteriorate. The cooler and darker your storage spot, the longer your herbs will last.

List of Brewing Herbs

For this section we have chosen only those brewing herbs that are known to be safe. Many plants used long ago in brewing are now considered to be toxic. Life is chancy enough without putting these in your beer.

We include each herb's common and botanical names, family, description and history, similar species that could be substituted for it in brewing, the best site for each herb, the parts used in brewing, when to harvest, propagation techniques, hardiness of each based on the USDA zone map, brewing uses, and the amount to use. Amounts listed in our herb profiles are suggestions based on fresh herbs for a 5-gallon (19 L) batch of beer.

You'll notice we include some fruit, and even trees, in our herb list. According to our working definition of brewing herbs, any plant besides hops used for bittering, flavoring, or aroma in beer qualifies as a brewing herb.

HARDINESS

Hardiness is the amount of cold a plant can tolerate. The zone map divides the United States and Canada up into hardiness zones, based on the minimum winter temperatures in each area. These are not average minimum temperatures; they are the absolute minimum temperatures that you can expect for a given area.

The zone map is only generally accurate. It doesn't take many gardening variables into account such as the number of frost-free days per year, the average rainfall, and the maximum summer temperature. All of these affect plant survival.

Perennial plants are given a rating for hardiness, based on the temperature range in which they can survive. But this rating isn't absolute. You can safely grow plants that are rated for your zone and lower numbered (colder) zones. Plants rated for zones 3 and 4 will have no trouble surviving zone 5 winters. Generally, if you give perennials a sheltered position, or if your yard is covered with an insulating blanket of snow all winter, you can get away with plants that are rated a zone or two warmer. Plants with hardiness ratings any higher than that should be potted up and brought inside for the winter. If you lose a plant that's supposed to survive in your zone, poor soil drainage is probably the culprit. Herbs don't like wet soil anytime, but especially in winter. Raising the soil level in your herb beds by 2 to 3 inches will improve winter survival rates. Your best source of information about the local climate is experienced gardeners and farmers who know your area well.

Herbs listed as hardy annuals can withstand quite a bit of frost; also, they often overwinter as self-sown seeds. Seeds for hardy annuals can be sown outside as soon as the soil can be worked in early spring. Half-hardy annuals can withstand light frost but are killed by repeated exposure to cold. They should not be sown outdoors before the frost-free date. Tender annuals are tropical plants that can be killed even by light frost. They should be planted after all danger of frost has passed, when the soil has warmed to at least 60°F. If you wish to overwinter tender annuals indoors, pot them up and bring them in well before the date of the first expected fall frost.

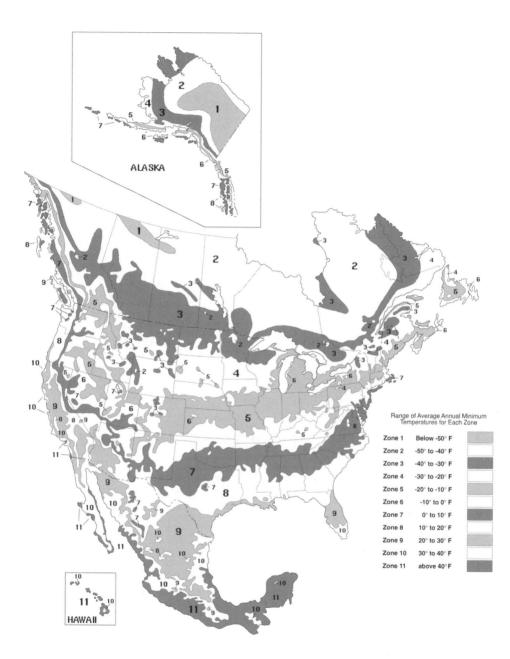

ALASKA

HAWAII

Range of Average Annual Minimum
Temperatures for Each Zone

Zone 1	Below -50° F
Zone 2	-50° to -40° F
Zone 3	-40° to -30° F
Zone 4	-30° to -20° F
Zone 5	-20° to -10° F
Zone 6	-10° to 0° F
Zone 7	0° to 10° F
Zone 8	10° to 20° F
Zone 9	20° to 30° F
Zone 10	30° to 40° F
Zone 11	above 40° F

Alecost

Chrysanthemum balsamita

Costmary, bible leaf

Family: Compositae (Daisy)

Description: Clump-forming perennial with narrow, serrated leaves to 7 inches (17 cm) long. Can grow to 4 feet (1.2 m) tall. Sometimes produces small yellow flowers in late summer. Its scent can range from being similar to balsam fir to oregano. Can be invasive once established. Very bitter.

Similar species: None

Hardiness: Zones 4 to 8

Best site: Fertile, well-drained soil in full sun to partial shade

Propagation: Division in spring, hardwood cuttings, seeds (but germination is poor)

Harvesting: Pick small quantities of leaves throughout the season to minimize stress to plants.

Brewing: Alecost was used to bitter ales in the 1600s. The leaves are very bitter, so they should not be used in combination with lots of hops. Use any amount from one sprig of leaves to 1 ounce (28 g) of leaves.

Anise Hyssop

Agastache foeniculum

Giant blue hyssop, licorice mint

Family: Labiatae (Mint)

Description: This native North American herb is neither an anise nor a hyssop, but a long-blooming, hardy mint with a flavor like licorice. It reaches a height of 3 to 4 feet (.9 to 1.2 m) with dark green, triangular leaves. It bears attractive spikes of blue-purple blooms from late June until frost.

Similar species: None

Hardiness: Zone 5 and up

Best site: This herb is native to moist woodlands but tolerates a range of conditions. Prefers moist, well-drained sandy loam. Full sun, but light shade will not bother it.

Propagation: Sow seeds outdoors in spring or fall, or propagate by division or softwood cuttings in spring. Anise hyssop blooms the first year from seeds and also self-sows readily.

Harvesting: Pick the leaves and the flowers when the plants first come into bloom.

Brewing: This herb is especially good in darker beers like porters and stouts. Use 1 ounce (28 g) of fresh leaves or flowers late in the boil to add a licorice-like flavor and aroma.

Basil

Ocimum basilicum

Sweet basil, Genovese basil

Family: Labiatae (Mint)

Description: Heat-loving, tender annual with smooth, oval leaves. The bushy, 1- to 2-foot-tall (.3 to .6 m) plant bears spikes of white to blue flowers in mid-summer.

Similar species: Cinnamon basil (*O. basilicum* 'Cinnamon') has purplish leaves and a spicy aroma; lemon basil *(O.b. citrodorum)* is used in Asian cooking; Mammoth basil (*O.b.* 'Mammoth Napoletano') is a large-leaved drying variety. There are many species and cultivars of basil to try in brewing.

Hardiness: Basil is a tender annual and always succumbs to the first fall frost.

Best site: Grows best in rich garden soil in full sun.

Propagation: Plant basil seeds indoors 10 to 12 weeks before the frost-free date. Transplant outdoors after all danger of frost has passed, when the weather is settled and nights are warm.

Harvesting: Pick the leaves throughout the season, whenever the plant has leaves to spare. Prune off the flower spikes to promote leaf growth.

Brewing: Although not a traditional brewing herb, basil has been finding its way into the brewpots of adventurous homebrewers for the past few years. Use 1 to 2 ounces (28 to 57 g) late in the boil to add a slightly bitter, spicy flavor and a clean, balsam scent to your beer.

Bee Balm

Monarda didyma

Bergamot, Oswego tea

Family: Labiatae (Mint)

Description: Vigorous, clump-forming perennial with dark green, hairy, triangular leaves. Grows 2 to 4 feet (.6 to 1.2 m) tall. Bears round, brilliant red, purple, or lavender blossoms in midsummer. As its name indicates, the plant is attractive to bees as well as hummingbirds and butterflies. Leaves have a menthol scent and astringent flavor.

Similar species: Mexican bergamot *(M. austromontana)*; lemon bee balm *(M. citriodora)*; wild bergamot *(M. fistulosa)* prefers dry, alkaline soil; spotted bee balm or horsemint *(M. punctata)* also prefers dry, alkaline soil. All the above are interchangeable with bee balm for brewing.

Hardiness: Zones 4 to 8

Best site: Rich, moist soil enriched with organic matter. Full sun to partial shade.

Propagation: Division in spring or fall, seeds

Harvesting: Harvest immediately after the flowers bloom. Cut the plant back to 1 inch (2.5 cm) from the ground to promote reblooming.

Brewing: The leaves of bee balm were used as a tea substitute during the American Revolutionary War. Use from one sprig to 1 ounce (28 g) of leaves and flowers at the end of the boil for a bitter, minty flavoring and menthol aroma.

Betony

Stachys officinalis

Woundwort

Family: Labiatae (Mint)

Description: Hardy perennial herb with hairy, notched, triangular leaves carried in pairs. Grows 2 to 3 feet (.6 to .9 m) tall. Bears spikes of small pink to red flowers in July and August.

Similar species: Not to be confused with lamb's-ears *(Stachys byzantina)*, which has furry, oval leaves.

Hardiness: Zones 4 to 9

Best site: Average soil. Full sun to partial shade.

Propagation: Division, cuttings, seeds

Harvesting: Harvest the leaves just before flowering.

Brewing: The bitter leaves were once used as a tea substitute. Use any amount from one sprig to 1 ounce (28 g) at start of boil for bittering.

PICKING INGREDIENTS OFF FRUIT TREES

Anyone lucky enough to own an apple tree (or crabapple, pear, persimmon, orange, mulberry, or cherry tree) will have a ready supply of brewing adjuncts. Your best bet is to press the fruit and collect a few gallons of juice for use as a brewing adjunct. You can also easily add the flavor of fruit to a 5 (19L) batch of beer by peeling and chopping 10 pounds (4.5 kg) of fruit and steeping them in the wort for 15 minutes after the boil ends.

Birch
Betula spp.

Sweet Birch, yellow birch, black birch

Family: Betulaceae (birch)

Description: Birches are a group of hardy, deciduous trees and shrubs grown for their attractive bark. Both yellow birches *(B. lutea)* and black birches *(B. lenta)* are referred to as sweet birches because their twigs give off a sweet, wintergreen scent when crushed. Yellow birch is a large tree with shaggy, gold to gray bark. Black birch has dark brown bark similar to that of a cherry tree. Black birch is more resistant to insects and diseases than any other birch.

Similar species: The sap of the paper birch *(B. papyrifera)* can be tapped as a brewing ingredient, but the twigs are too astringent tasting to brew with.

Hardiness: Zones 4 to 7

Best site: Well-drained or slightly sandy, loamy soil. Full sun to partial shade.

Propagation: Planting a young sapling is recommended. Trees should be planted in autumn. Be careful to cut away any roots that circle the trunk; birches are prone to root-girdling, where the tree's own roots literally strangle it.

Harvesting: Young, new-growth twigs can be cut anytime during the growing season. In early spring, sweet birches can also be tapped with a drill, spigot, and pail for their sap. Birch sap can be used to replace water in any beer recipe.

Brewing: Records of using birch in beer go back to the eighteenth century. Use ¼ to 6 ounces (7 to 170 g) of twigs late in the boil to give a wintergreen flavor and scent to your beer. Up to 5 gallons of birch sap can be used in place of water for birch beer.

Blackberry

Rubus spp.

Brambleberry, thimbleberry, cloudberry, dewberry

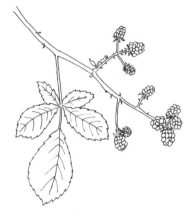

Family: Rosaceae (Rose)

Description: A bramble fruit growing on 4-to 6-foot-high (1.2 to 1.8 m) canes that are usually, but not always, covered in thorns. It is both cultivated and found growing wild. It is a tender perennial with flowers blooming in May and June followed by big, juicy, black fruits.

Similar species: Raspberry *(Rubus idaeus)*

Hardiness: Zones 4 to 8

Best site: A site sheltered from excessive wind with good air circulation and plenty of sun. The soil should be rich in organic matter to assure good moisture retention and good drainage. Do not plant blackberries near raspberries or where tomatoes, eggplants, or peppers have previously grown since they are susceptible to verticillium wilt.

Propagation: Buying virus-free nursery stock is the best way to insure disease-free crops. To increase your stock, select strong suckers in the fall after they have become dormant. Dig them up and carefully replant them in a new bed. Plant new canes in early spring or fall in a trench 2 to 3 inches (5 to 7.6 cm) deep spaced 15 to 18 inches (38 to 46 cm) apart. Water and mulch well.

Harvesting: Pick the berries when they are completely ripe. During the harvest season, the bushes will need daily picking. The berries are very delicate and need to be used or frozen soon after picking; otherwise they will deteriorate. Do not wash the berries. Instead, gently pour them out into a pan and pick out any debris before using.

Brewing: A longtime favorite of brewers. Use 6 to 10 pounds (2.7 to 4.5 kg) of blackberries in fruit beer or in mead.

Blessed Thistle

Cnicus benedictus

Carduus, St. Benedict's thistle

Family: Compositae (Daisy)

Description: This sprawling, Mediterranean annual has spiky, down-covered leaves like those of the dandelion. It bears small, yellow flowers in late spring and grows 18 inches to 2 feet (46 to 60 cm) high.

Similar species: None

Hardiness: Tender annual

Best site: Moist, well-drained loam amended with compost. Full sun.

Propagation: Plant seeds indoors in early spring or sow outside on the frost-free date for your region. A short cold treatment increases germination of seeds planted indoors. Sow the seeds ¼ to ½ inch (6 to 12 mm) deep, water, seal the pot in a freezer bag, and put it in the refrigerator or a cold outbuilding for three to seven days. Bring the pot back inside to a warm spot to germinate. Transplant the seedlings outdoors after all danger of frost has passed. Self-sows readily in mild climates, but the seeds will not survive in areas with harsh winters.

Harvesting: Harvest the whole plant at midsummer after blooming or in early fall before the first frost.

Brewing: Historically the leaves of blessed thistle were used as a hop substitute to bitter ale in Europe. Use 2 ounces to 1 pound (58 to 454 g) of fresh, cleaned plants early in the boil for bittering.

Borage

Borago officinalis

Beebread, star flower

Family: Boraginaceae (Borage)

Description: A coarse, drooping hardy annual with oval, bristly leaves. It bears five-pointed star-shaped, intense blue flowers in midsummer and grows 2 to 3 feet (.6 to .9 m) high. Attractive to bees. Sometimes flowers the second year.

Similar species: Salad burnet *(Poterium sanguisorba)* may be substituted.

Hardiness: Hardy annual

Best site: Moist, light, neutral soil enriched with composted manure. Full sun. Also can be grown indoors in a pot.

Propagation: Sow the seeds outside as soon as the soil can be worked in spring. Borage also self-sows enthusiastically, but doesn't become a weed as young seedlings are easy to pull.

Harvesting: Pick the flowers when they first come into bloom; pick the leaves throughout the season.

Brewing: Borage must be used fresh; it doesn't dry successfully. Use any amount from one fresh sprig to 2 ounces (57 g), at the end of the boil for a spicy, cucumber-like flavor and aroma. Traditionally this herb was steeped in wine and said to increase courage and cause merriment.

Chamomile

Chamaemelum nobile

Roman chamomile

Family: Compositae (Daisy)

Description: Low growing, spreading perennial with fernlike
foliage. Bears tiny, daisylike flowers
in late spring through late summer.
These have an apple-like scent. Prefers
cool climates. Often escapes cultivation and can be wild gathered.

Similar species: German chamomile
(Matricaria recutita) is a 2- to 3-foot tall
(.6 to .9 m), self-sowing annual. It produces
more blossoms per season than Roman chamomile but is otherwise interchangeable.

Hardiness: Zones 4 to 8

Best site: Neutral or slightly acidic sandy soil to rich loam. Full sun
to partial shade.

Propagation: Seeds should be planted outdoors as early in spring as
the soil can be worked. Can also be propagated from offset cuttings in spring.

Harvesting: Pick the flowers when the petals turn back. Can be harvested often. Flower production may drop off in areas with hot
summers.

Brewing: This traditional tea herb is said to be one of the secret
ingredients in Celis White, an award-winning Belgian White beer
from Austin, Texas. Although mild when steeped, chamomile
becomes surprisingly bitter when boiled, which accounts for its
historical popularity with brewers of Purl and Mumm. Use ¼ to
2 ounces (7 to 57 g) of fresh flowers at the end of the boil for an
apple-like flavoring and aroma or at the beginning of the boil for
bitterness.

Clary Sage

Salvia sclarea

Clary, clear-eye

Family: Labiatae (Mint)

Description: Biennial with broad, heart-shaped, dull green, fuzzy leaves. Grows to a height of 3 to 5 feet (.9 to 1.5 m). Bears spikes of white to lilac-blue flowers in June or July of its second year. Whole plant is very fragrant. Can be grown as an annual if started early enough.

Similar species: See Sage (page 97)

Hardiness: Zones 4 to 9. In areas with cold winters and unreliable snow cover, the plant should be mulched to help it survive winter.

Best site: Average to sandy, well-drained or dry soil. Full sun.

Propagation: Seeds should be sown outdoors on the frost-free date. Clary sage can be grown as an annual if seeds are started early indoors and transplanted outside. Division can also be used.

Harvesting: Pick flowers just after blooming. Leaves can be picked throughout the season.

Brewing: Clary sage was used as a hop substitute by German brewers in the sixteenth century. Along with elder flowers, clary sage blossoms are used to flavor Muscatel wine. Use from one sprig to 2 ounces (57 g) of fresh flowers to add a bitter flavor and a balsamlike aroma.

Coriander

Coriandrum sativum

Cilantro, Chinese parsley (leaves), coriander (seeds)

Family: Umbelliferae (Carrot)

Description: Bright green annual with lobed leaves. Bears clusters of white to reddish flowers in late spring or summer. Its pink pollen is attractive to bees.

Similar species: Epazote *(Chenopodium ambrosioides)* may be substituted for leaves; no substitute for seeds.

Hardiness: Hardy annual

Best site: Rich, light, well-drained, neutral to slightly alkaline soil. Full sun to partial shade.

Propagation: Plant seeds outdoors as early in the spring as the soil can be worked, since the plants produce best in cool weather. Soaking the seeds overnight in warm water improves germination. Coriander also self-sows and may become weedy in areas over time.

Harvesting: Pick the leaves before the flowers bloom in late spring. Gather the seeds after they have turned brown, but before seeds scatter.

Brewing: The seeds are a traditional ingredient in Belgian White beers and many holiday ales. They have a sweet, clovelike flavor. The fresh leaves have a strong, distinctive scent and flavor used as a regular ingredient in Mexican and Chinese cooking. Use from one sprig to one ounce (28 g) of fresh leaves or ¼ to 2 ounces (7 to 57 g) of seeds at the beginning of the boil for flavoring.

Dandelion

Taraxacum officinale

Lion's tooth, yellow gowan, Irish daisy

Family: Compositae (Daisy)

Description: Dandelion is a
plant that needs no
introduction, but it might
need a re-introduction.
This herbaceous perennial
with jagged-toothed leaves
and a long taproot, the bane of
many lawn owners, is not the useless
weed most think. This bitter-tasting plant
has been used throughout history as a
medicinal plant and brewing herb.

Similar species: None

Hardiness: Zones 2 to 9

Best site: Any soil. Full sun to partial shade.

Propagation: You can grow dandelions from seeds, but more likely
than not you can find enough of this plant in your lawn or in
the wild.

Harvesting: The entire plant should be pulled out of the ground
when the flowers open. If harvesting from a lawn, first make sure
the grass hasn't been sprayed with a herbicide or pesticide.

Brewing: How many dandelions to use depends on the time of year.
In early spring, before the flowers have appeared, dandelion
greens are fairly mild. But later on when the plants are large and
milky, they become increasingly bitter. You should not use dandelions taken from a lawn where any chemicals have been used. Use
anywhere between 2 ounces and 1 pound (57 to 454 g) early in
the boil for bittering.

Elder

Sambucus nigra

European elder, common elder, elderflower, elderberry

Family: Caprifoliaceae
(Honeysuckle)

Description: Hardy, deciduous
shrub that branches from its
base. It bears clusters of white
flowers in May or June, followed by dark purple fruits in
late summer. Height and spread
20 feet (6 m).

Similar species: American elder
(Sambucus canadensis), with a height
and spread 12 feet (3.6 m), is hardy
to zone 4.

Hardiness: Zones 4 to 9

Best site: Moist garden soil. Full sun.

Propagation: Take cuttings in autumn from the shoots that sprout
prolifically from the roots; root cuttings can also be used. Seeds
will take several years to grow into a blooming plant. Shrubs need
to be pruned every spring.

Harvesting: Harvest flowers when they open. Berries are best picked
when they are fully ripe, after a light frost if possible.

Brewing: Elder flowers have long been used in brewing as a flavoring
herb. The berries are also used in cooking, jellies, and wine. Elder
requires a warning: Although the flowers and berries are edible,
the bark and leaves are poisonous and shouldn't be eaten. Use
2 ounces (57 g) of the flowers for dry hopping. Use 1 to 6 pounds
(.45 to 2.7 kg) of the berries to add a sweet, honeylike flavor to a
fruit beer.

Elecampane *Inula helenium*

Wild sunflower, Inula, elf-dock

Family: Compositae (Daisy)

Description: Large, coarse perennial
with bristly leaves to 2 feet long.
Grows 4 to 6 feet (1.2 to 1.8 m) tall.
Bears yellow, 3- to 4-inch (7 to
10 cm), sunflowerlike blossoms
from June to August. Flowers
smell slightly of honey.

Similar species: Giant Inula *(Inula mag-
nifica)*, Swordleaf Inula *(Inula ensifolia)*

Hardiness: Zones 3 to 8

Best site: Moist, moderately fertile clay soil.
Full sun to full shade. Deeply dug soil
will produce vigorous plants with large roots.

Propagation: The plant can be grown from seeds started indoors
about seven weeks before the frost-free date, or propagated from
root cuttings when the roots are harvested in fall. Be sure each
root cutting has an "eye," or new bud, at the top.

Harvesting: After the first frost, gather roots from plants at least two
years old.

Brewing: Elecampane has a long history as a brewing ingredient
and medicinal herb. Only the roots are used in brewing. They
provide a sweet flavor similar to licorice. Use ¼ to 2 ounces
(7 to 57 g) of the dried root midway through the boil to add the
licorice flavor.

Gentian

Gentiana lutea

Yellow gentian

Family: Gentianaceae (Gentian)

Description: A tall perennial with large, stiff, oval, dark green leaves and large roots. Bears clusters of large, yellow flowers in July and August.

Similar species: Stemless gentian *(G. angustifolia)* is a blue-flowered dwarf, 4 to 6 inches (10 to 15 cm) tall, that needs alkaline soil, zone 6. Closed gentian *(G. andrewsii)* is also blue-flowered, 2 feet (.6 m) tall, native, likes acidic soil, zone 5.

Hardiness: Zones 7 to 8

Best site: Moist, well-drained, peaty soil with an alkalinizing additive in it such as lime. Full sun to partial shade. Gentians prefer a cool, moist climate like that of the Pacific Northwest.

Propagation: Best propagated by division or root cuttings in the spring. It is difficult to grow gentians from seed. Germination is poor and the seeds require at least two months of cold treatment. Some seeds may take as long as four years to sprout!

Harvesting: Harvest the roots in the late summer or early autumn.

Brewing: Gentian roots have long been used in Sweden to bitter beer. The roots are very bitter and act as flavoring agent in Angostura bitters and Moxie soda. Be careful when brewing with this herb. Unlike many other brewing herbs, the flavor of gentian does not mellow over time. We recommend using a maximum of 1 teaspoon (⅛ ounce or 3.5 g) of dried root early in the boil for bittering.

DUBIOUS BREWING HERBS

Some herbs that have been used traditionally in brewing have been found to be poisonous or otherwise hazardous to human health. However, many of them are attractive and interesting when grown as ornamental plants; growing a few of these is a great way to connect with the history of brewing. They are perfectly safe to look at, and many are worthy garden residents.

Angelica is an "iffy" herb, and some would probably object to its appearance in this list of dangerous or dubious plants. It is one of the dozen herbs used to flavor gin. It is included here mainly because we decided to err on the side of caution.

Angelica   *(Angelica archangelica)*

Danger: Suspected carcinogen, mutagen.

Sweet Gale or Bog myrtle   *(Myrica gale)*

Danger: Suspected carcinogen.

Comfrey   *(Symphytum officinale)*

Danger: Suspected carcinogen.

Mugwort   *(Artemisia vulgaris)*

Danger: Poisonous. Banned by United States Food and Drug Administration for internal use.

Pennyroyal   *(Mentha pulegium)*

Danger: Poisonous if taken internally.

Tansy   *(Tanacetum vulgare)*

Danger: Poisonous if taken internally; can be lethal in large doses.

Thorn apple   *(Datura stramonium)*

Danger: Very poisonous. Contact poison; wear gloves when handling. Can be lethal if eaten.

Wormwood   *(Artemisia absinthium)*

Danger: Poisonous if taken internally. Causes convulsions in large doses. Central nervous system poison.

Ginger

Zingiber officinale

Family: Zingiberaceae (Ginger)

Description: This well-known spice is a bamboo-like tropical perennial with long, grassy leaves and a knotty tuber. In frost-free areas, ginger can grow to a height of 5 feet (1.5 m).

Similar species: Galangal or Siamese ginger *(Alpinia galanga)* is an unrelated, but similar-tasting, spice that may be substituted in brewing. In fact, nineteenth-century English brewers of Purl preferred galangal to ginger in their brews.

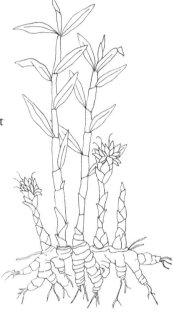

Hardiness: Zone 9 and up. Outside the tropics, ginger can be successfully grown in a pot indoors. Plant the tubers shallowly in a mix of equal parts loam, sand, peat moss, and compost. Ginger requires warmth, moisture, and humidity to thrive. During the summer, harden off the plant and move the pot outside to a partially shady location.

Best site: Fertile, moist, well-drained soil. Partial shade.

Propagation: Roots can be divided and replanted at harvest.

Harvesting: You can cut the root 8 to 12 months after planting.

Brewing: Ginger has always been a standard ale-brewing ingredient. It's only been a few decades since the major English breweries stopped using it. If you don't want to grow it yourself, fresh ginger can be found at many health food stores and increasingly at super-markets. Add ¼ to 6 ounces (7 to 171 g) of grated gingerroot at the beginning of the boil depending on how strong a flavor you want in your brew.

Ginseng *Panax ssp.*

Family: Araliaceae (Aralia or Ginseng)

Description: Ginseng is a hardy perennial with shiny, dark green leaves. It grows to a height of about 15 inches (.4 m). Tiny, greenish white flowers appear in early summer, followed by bright red berries with two seeds each. Ginseng is grown for its large, spreading, tuberous roots.

Similar species: American ginseng *(Panax quinquefolius)*, dwarf ginseng *(Panax trifolius)*, and Chinese ginseng *(Panax ginseng)* can all be used for brewing.

Hardiness: Zones 3 to 6

Best site: Grows best in light-textured, humusy loam, preferably on a south-facing, rocky slope with 75 percent shade. Fertile, moist, well-drained soil.

Propagation: Harvest the fruits from mature plants, soak them in water for 24 hours, and bury them in a well-marked spot. Dig them up the following spring and check for germination. Germination can take from 3 to 18 months. Seeds require cold treatment; pre-treated seeds are available from some mail-order catalogs. Year-old ginseng seedlings are also available from some nursery sources. The seedlings should be planted outdoors in early autumn.

Harvesting: Ginseng roots are harvested in the fall of their fifth year. Rinse the roots off with a hose and spread them out to dry. Drying time varies and can take as long as a month depending on the weather.

Brewing: Ginseng has become increasingly popular as a brewing ingredient with homebrewers and microbrewers. Use ¼ to 2 ounces (7 to 57 g) late in the boil for tangy flavoring.

Greek Oregano

Origanum vulgare subsp.
hirta, Origanum heracleoticum

Italian oregano

Family: Labiatae (Mint)

Description: This vigorous,
spreading perennial has
slightly hairy, fragrant, oval-
shaped, greenish-gray leaves. Bears
small clusters of white flowers from
midsummer to early fall.

Similar species: A good deal of confusion sur-
rounds Greek oregano, most familiar as a pizza
and spaghetti sauce herb. Common oregano
(O. vulgare) is bland, less aromatic, and less useful
in brewing or cooking. Sweet marjoram *(O. majorana)* is also
related and is a traditional brewing herb in porter.

Hardiness: Zones 4 and up

Best site: Grows best in rich, well-drained, moist soil in full sun.

Propagation: Easily grown from seeds, by division, or from cuttings.
However, the plants vary a great deal when grown from seeds. We
recommend obtaining a plant or a cutting from someone with an
established bed.

Harvesting: Pick the leaves throughout the season. Greek oregano
can be cut back often, since it's very enthusiastic once established.

Brewing: This traditional culinary herb is increasingly finding its way
into the brewpots of both professional and home brewers. Use
2 ounces (57 g) late in the boil to add a spicy flavor and aroma to
your beer. The same amount can also be dry hopped in the secondary fermenter to add a strong, distinctive smell to your batch.

Heather
Calluna vulgaris

Scotch heather, ling

Family: Ericaceae (Heath)

Description: Low-growing, mat-forming perennial ground cover with tiny leaves. Bears short spikes of pink to lavender flowers from summer to early fall. Prone to Japanese beetles and root rot. Grows 6 inches to 3 feet (.15 to .9 m) tall.

Similar species: Spring heath *(Erica carnea)* is a low-growing, evergreen shrub with white to red blossoms. Interchangeable with heather in brewing.

Hardiness: Zones 4 to 7

Best site: Moist, well-drained, peaty, acidic soil. Full sun. Prefers a cool climate.

Propagation: Propagate the plants from offshoots in summer, or by seed.

Harvesting: Pick the flowers after they open.

Brewing: Heather ale is an ancient Scottish specialty that was brewed well into the late nineteenth century and is now experiencing a revival. It supposedly originated with the Picts, the small, dark, pre-Celtic people of Britain. Heather imparts a spicy, complex bitterness and a deep purple color to beer. Use 1 to 5 cups (.2 to 1.1 L) of flowers late in the boil for flavoring and aroma. Add one more cup (.2 L) of flowers dry hopped during the fermentation stage for a purple color and a strong heather flavor.

Horehound

Marrubium vulgare

Hoarhound

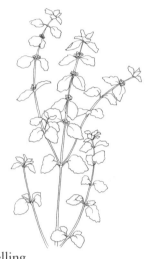

Family: Labiatae (Mint)

Description: Branching perennial with woolly, gray-green, serrated leaves and woolly stems. Bears tiny white flowers tucked at the bases of leaves in summer.

Similar species: White woolly horehound *(Marrubium incanum)* is woollier; interchangeable with horehound for brewing. So-called black horehound *(Ballota nigra)* is a foul-smelling member of the same family and should not be used for brewing.

Hardiness: Zones 4 to 8. In areas with cold winters and unreliable snow cover, horehound plantings should be mulched to help them survive winter.

Best site: Poor, sandy, dry, alkaline soil. Full sun.

Propagation: Seeds can be sown where the plants are to grow in autumn or as early in spring as the soil can be worked. Horehound can also be propagated by division or softwood cuttings. Established plantings spread by root runners and self-sowing, but not aggresively.

Harvesting: Pick the leaves and flowers when the plant comes into bloom. Horehound usually doesn't bloom the first year from seed. Harvest only the top third of first-year plants if they do bloom.

Brewing: The fresh herb is very bitter. It adds a warming, almost menthol finish to beer. Horehound ale was a specialty of the English midlands. This herb has a long medicinal history as well; it is still used in the making of cough drops. Use 2 ounces (57 g) of fresh leaves and flowers at the start of the boil for bittering. Cut the quantity to only 1 ounce (28 g) if dried horehound is used.

Hyssop

Hyssopus officinalis

Family: Labiatae (Mint)

Description: Compact, woody, shrublike perennial with small, spiky leaves. Bears spikes of blue to purple flowers in summer. Attractive to bees.

Similar species: None

Hardiness: Zones 6 to 9

Best site: Light, dry, limey soil. Full sun to partial shade. In moist, rich soil it loses the essential oils that give the herb its flavor and aroma. It also dislikes humidity. In very hot regions, it benefits from partial shade.

Propagation: Seeds can be sown where the plants are to grow in early spring, or plants can be propagated by cuttings and division. The plants should be divided every three to five years to prevent them from becoming woody, and to keep them blooming.

Harvesting: Pick the leaves and flowers when the blossoms open.

Brewing: Historically, hyssop has been used as a medicinal tea in addition to being a brewing ingredient. Today, it's a flavoring agent in liqueurs such as Benedictine and Chartreuse. Use 1 ounce (28 g) of fresh leaves during the early boil for a menthol flavor. Dry hopping with the same amount will give your beer a minty, medicinal scent.

Juniper
Juniperus communis

Common juniper

Family: Cupressaceae (Cypress)

Description: Perennial evergreen shrub
with either a low-spreading or tall,
branching form. Height usually 2 to
6 feet (.6 to 1.8 m). Its needlelike foliage
varies from dull green to silvery blue; its
bark is reddish and thin. Plants are
dioecious, having male and female
flowers on separate plants; both are
needed to produce berries. Plants flower
from spring to early summer; male flowers are yellow, females
green. Berries are green ripening to purple-blue the second year.

Similar species: There are many *hybrids* and *cultivars* of juniper.
Shore juniper *(J. conferta)* is a low-growing, salt-tolerant shrub,
hardy to zone 6. Creeping juniper *(J. horizontalis)* is a mat-forming shrub, hardy to zone 3.

Hardiness: Zones 3 to 6

Best site: Well-drained, sandy loam. Full sun. In a shady or sheltered
location, the plants are less fragrant.

Propagation: Juniper can be propagated from seeds, but germination
may take up to two years. Cuttings are a more reliable method.
Transplant new seedlings in early spring or autumn.

Harvesting: Pick the berries starting in the second year, after they
turn color; the needles can be picked throughout the season.

Brewing: Juniper's piney foliage and pungent berries have been used
to flavor traditional ales in the Netherlands for centuries, as well
as liquors such as gin. Use 1 to 2 tablespoons (15 to 30 ml) of
fresh berries late in the boil for a ginlike flavor. The leaves, 1 to 4
ounces (28 to 114 g), can be added to the secondary fermenter to
give your beer a bittersweet aroma.

Lavender

Lavandula angustifolia

True lavender, English lavender

Family: Labiatae (Mint)

Description: Branching, shrublike perennial with grayish, fragrant, needlelike leaves. Purplish-mauve spikes of flowers bloom in summer.

Similar species: Spike lavender (*L. latifolia*) is interchangeable with English lavender.

Hardiness: Zones 6 to 9. Needs to be wrapped or mulched during winter if planted in an exposed location in the colder zones.

Best site: Well-drained slightly acid to slightly alkaline soil (pH 6.4 to 8.3). Full sun.

Propagation: Propagation is usually by division or cuttings in spring. Harder to grow from seeds, since germination is often slow and irregular, and some forms will not come true from seeds. Use a light, soilless mix without peat for cuttings.

Harvesting: Cut leaves and flowers 6 inches (15 cm) below the flower spikes just as blooms open.

Brewing: Although now chiefly known as a potpourri and cosmetics herb, lavender has a history as a brewing ingredient dating back at least to the 1600s. Needless to say, the herb does not taste like it smells. Instead it contributes a complex bitterness much like that of heather. Use ½ ounce (14 g) of fresh or dried flowers late in the boil. The flowers can also be used for dry hopping.

Lemon Balm

Melissa officinalis

Sweet balm, balm

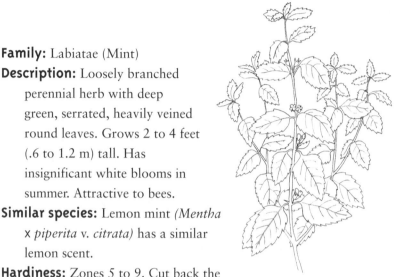

Family: Labiatae (Mint)

Description: Loosely branched perennial herb with deep green, serrated, heavily veined round leaves. Grows 2 to 4 feet (.6 to 1.2 m) tall. Has insignificant white blooms in summer. Attractive to bees.

Similar species: Lemon mint *(Mentha* x *piperita* v. *citrata)* has a similar lemon scent.

Hardiness: Zones 5 to 9. Cut back the whole plant to 2 inches (5 cm) above the ground for the winter. May require winter protection; not reliably cold-hardy in zone 5.

Best site: Average to poor, well-drained, limey soil. Full sun to shade.

Propagation: Division in spring, cuttings, or seeds. Sow seeds where the plants are to stand in early spring or autumn. The plants also self-sow once established.

Harvesting: Cut the leaves just before plants flower. The leaves should be used fresh or dried immediately after harvest; otherwise they turn black and lose their flavor and smell.

Brewing: Like many of the brewing herbs, lemon balm is noted for its mild sedative quality. According to seventeenth-century herbalist Nicholas Culpepper, it "causeth the mind and heart to become merry, and driveth away all troublesome cares." Also known as a traditional wine herb, lemon balm is used today to flavor many liqueurs. Use ½ ounce (14 g) of the fresh leaves late in the boil to add a strong lemon scent and flavor.

Licorice   *Glycyrrhiza glabra*

Family: Leguminosae (Pea)

Description: Branching perennial
with small, oblong, yellow-green
leaves. Pea-like, ½-inch-long,
purple to lavender flowers in midsummer. The plant can grow up to 7 feet tall.
It produces a long taproot with spreading
runners.

Similar species: Russian or German licorice
(Glycyrrhiza echinata) is interchangeable with *G. glabra.*

Hardiness: Zones 7 to 10. Gardeners in colder zones can grow
potted licorice outside during the summer and bring the plants
inside to overwinter them.

Best site: Rich, moist, deeply prepared, sandy garden soil. Full sun.
In the wild, licorice often grows on streambanks, where it benefits
from frequent floods.

Propagation: Can be propagated by root cuttings or softwood cuttings in spring. The seeds are hard-shelled and benefit from soaking in hot water. Place the seeds in a teacup and cover them with
boiling water. Leave them to soak until they have swollen to
about twice their original size. Drain the seeds and plant them
shallowly in a pot. Transplant seedlings outside after all danger of
frost has passed.

Harvesting: Roots can be cut in late autumn when the plants are at
least three years old.

Brewing: Licorice has a long history as a brewing ingredient. Licorice
contributes a sweet flavor and long-lasting head to beer. The characteristic flavor of licorice candy comes from anise, not licorice
root. Use ¼ ounce (7 g) of dried root at the start of the boil to add
the sweet flavor to dark ales like porter and stout.

Milk Thistle

Silybum marianum

Mary's milk thistle

Family: Compositae (Daisy)

Description: Striking annual with
dark green, spiny leaves mottled
with white. Bears spiky, purplish rose blooms in late
summer. Attractive to
bees. Grows 4 to 6 feet (1.2
to 1.8 m) tall and almost as broad in
fertile soil. Widespread roadside weed,
especially in the Pacific Northwest and
northern California. Easily gathered
from the wild.

Similar species: Blessed thistle *(Cnicus benedictus)* can be substituted as a brewing ingredient. (See p. 69.)

Hardiness: Hardy annual

Best site: Can tolerate dry soil but does best in well-drained, rich
garden soil. Full sun.

Propagation: Seeds should be planted ¼ inch deep in the soil in early
spring or fall. Milk thistle's seeds are borne on parachutes like
those of dandelions, so the plants self-sow unpredictably.

Harvesting: Collect seeds when they ripen but before seedhead shat-
ters. Pick leaves and stems throughout the season. Milk thistle has
large, sharp thorns, so wear gloves when harvesting.

Brewing: Milk thistle's bitter flavoring has been used historically
in many European beers to offset the sweetness of malt. Use
2 ounces (57 g) of the seeds or fresh leaves and stems early in
the boil for bittering.

Mint

Mentha spp.

Family: Labiatae (Mint)

Description: Mints are a group of over 20 species of upright perennials with an unmistakable aroma and refreshing taste. Spearmint grows to 2½ feet (72 cm) high, with smooth stems and 2-inch-long (5 cm), toothed leaves. Peppermint grows to 3 feet (90 cm) high and spreads by means of runners traveling over the soil surface. Apple mint grows to 4 feet (1.2 m) tall, with oval, hairy leaves.

Similar species: Spearmint *(M. spicata)*, peppermint *(M. x piperita)*, and apple mint *(M. suaveolens)* can be substituted as brewing ingredients.

Hardiness: Zones 4 to 9

Best site: Mints grow best in moist, rich garden soil with a pH range of 6.0 to 7.0. Full sun to partial shade. All are potentially invasive, spreading by runners. It's a good idea to confine mints to their own bed or grow it in containers to keep the plants in bounds.

Propagation: Propagation is by seed (except peppermint), stem cuttings, or cuttings of runners. Because of mint's tendency to cross between species, it's wise to begin with plants or cuttings of a known variety.

Harvesting: Harvest mints as they come into bloom. Cut back the plants to about 6 inches (15 cm) from the ground and hang to dry.

Brewing: Use up to 2 ounces (57 g) of fresh leaves or 1 ounce (28 g) of dried leaves late in the boil for aroma and flavoring. The same amount of leaves can also be added during secondary fermentation for a stronger minty aroma to your ale.

Nasturtium

Tropaeolum majus

Indian cress

Family: Tropaeolaceae
(Nasturtium)

Description: These trailing, tender
annuals are easily grown. They
bear trumpetlike, yellow to deep
red flowers beneath flat, circular leaves.
In favorable conditions they may spread
2 to 3 feet (.6 to .9 m) and mound up to
a foot high. In frost-free areas they can
bloom all year. Check the blossoms
for earwigs, which often shelter there.
The plants are very tender, dying at the first sign of frost.

Similar species: None

Hardiness: Tender annual

Best site: Prefer a soil that is nitrogen poor and adequately watered
in full sun. Too much nitrogen tends to produce many leaves
and few blossoms. Nasturtiums are easily grown in containers.
They do poorly when transplanted, so use a large enough pot to
allow growth.

Propagation: Sow seeds after all danger of frost has passed, when
the soil has warmed to at least 65°F (18°C). In warm climates, the
plants will self-sow readily.

Harvesting: Harvest the blooms and leaves throughout the season.

Brewing: For a long time nasturtiums have been popular in salads
and teas. Homebrewers are increasingly dropping the edible
leaves and flowers into their brew kettles to add a unique, peppery aroma and taste to their beer. Use 5 to 10 cups (1.2 to 2.4 L)
of the fresh flowers and leaves late in the boil.

Nettles

Urtica dioica

Stinging nettle

Family: Urticaceae (Nettle)

Description: Single-stalked, bushy perennial with heart-shaped leaves covered
with tiny prickles that sting on contact.
Bears tiny clusters of greenish flowers
from July to September. Reputed to
improve flavor of aromatic herbs when
grown nearby by helping to boost their
essential oil content. A common weed of
waste places, easily gathered from the wild.
Grows 4 to 6 feet (1.2 to 1.8 m) tall.

Similar species: Dwarf nettle *(Urtica urens)* is
an annual nettle under 1 foot (30 cm) tall.

Hardiness: Zones 3 to 9

Best site: Rich, moist to damp soil. Full sun to partial shade. Wild nettles are often found at the edge of woods or pastures or near water.

Propagation: Sow seeds indoors 12 weeks before the frost-free date.
Transplant seedlings outside as soon as the soil can be worked.
The plants can also be propagated by cuttings or division after the
tops have died back in fall. Handle the divisions carefully with
gloves, since the roots can also sting.

Harvesting: Wear gloves when harvesting. Leaves should be cut
before the plants flower, generally in late spring.

Brewing: Nettles are related to hops, and nettle beer used to be
common in England. Fresh nettles are best handled with gloves,
but plants lose the ability to sting when dried or cooked. Use
2 ounces (57 g) of dried nettle leaves or up to ½ pound (272 g) of
fresh nettles at the start of the boil for bittering.

Raspberry

Rubus idaeus

Red Raspberry

Family: *Rosaceae* (Rose)

Description: A shrubby, biennial
bramble fruit growing on thorny
canes up to 6 feet (1.8 m) tall. It is
both cultivated and found growing wild.
Small white flowers bloom starting in the
second year followed by deep red, seedy
fruit. Raspberries come in two classes:
summer-bearing and everbearing. Summer-bearers ripen a single crop
in midsummer; everbearers ripen one crop in early summer and
another in fall. In areas with severe winters or short growing seasons, everbearers may never ripen the second crop. Beware —
Japanese beetles love raspberry plants.

Similar species: Blackberry (*Rubus* spp.)

Hardiness: Zones 4 to 8

Best site: A sheltered site with good air circulation and plenty of sun.
The soil should be rich in organic matter to assure good moisture
retention and good drainage. Avoid planting where tomatoes, eggplants, or peppers had previously grown since they are susceptible
to verticillium wilt.

Propagation: Buy virus-free nursery stock to insure disease-free crops.
To increase your stock, select strong suckers in the fall after they
have become dormant. Dig them up and carefully replant them in a
new bed. Plant new canes in early spring or fall in a trench 2 to 3
inches (5 to 8 cm) deep spaced 15 to 18 inches (38 to 46 cm) apart.

Harvesting: During the harvest season, the bushes will need daily picking. The berries are delicate and need to be used or frozen soon after
picking to prevent deterioration. Do not wash the berries. Instead,
pour them into a pan and pick out any debris.

Brewing: A longtime favorite of brewers. Use 6 to 10 pounds (2.7 to
4.5 kg) of berries in fruit beer or in mead.

Rhubarb *Rheum* x *cultorum*

Family: Polygonacecae (Buckwheat)

Description: This long-lived perennial
can grow to a height of 30 inches
(76 cm) and spread up to 6 feet
(1.8 m). The ruffled, prickly
leaves can be as much as
18 inches (45 cm) across, and
the smooth, thick stems can
be up to 2 feet (.6 m) long.

Similar species: None

Hardiness: Zones 2 to 7. Rhubarb is extremely cold tolerant. It will
survive down to –50°F (–46°C), but it can't endure warm climates. It needs a dormant period of cold to continue producing
year after year.

Best site: Rhubarb grows best in rich, well-manured, moist garden
soil in full sun.

Propagation: Rhubarb is propagated from the roots. Dig up a
mature plant (at least three years old) and carefully separate the
roots. Plant "sets" or individual roots in the fall, 1½ to 2 feet
(45 to 60 cm) apart, with the visible buds at soil level. Roots are
thick but brittle, and they snap easily. Mulch the beds thoroughly
to protect against frost damage.

Harvesting: Harvest the rhubarb stems in late spring and early
summer while they are young and tender. Carefully pull the stems
up from the base, and they will break cleanly off the plant. Harvest
only lightly the first year after planting; in subsequent years, harvest heavily until the stem quality declines in midsummer.

Brewing: The rhubarb's fleshy stems have been used in brewing since
the Middle Ages and give beer a pungent sweet-sourness unlike
ordinary fruit. Use 5 to 10 pounds (2.3 to 4.5 kg) of fresh stems
for brewing a truly unusual fruit beer.

Rose Hips

Rosa rugosa

Wild rose, beach rose, rugosa rose

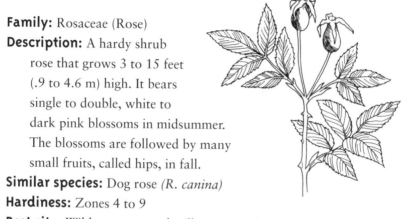

Family: Rosaceae (Rose)

Description: A hardy shrub rose that grows 3 to 15 feet (.9 to 4.6 m) high. It bears single to double, white to dark pink blossoms in midsummer. The blossoms are followed by many small fruits, called hips, in fall.

Similar species: Dog rose *(R. canina)*

Hardiness: Zones 4 to 9

Best site: Wild roses can and will grow on almost any site, anywhere. They will endure heat, cold, dryness, salt, and clay or sandy soil. Given a rich, well-drained, loamy soil in full sun they will flourish.

Propagation: Can be grown readily from seeds, but the most reliable method is softwood cuttings.

Harvesting: Wild rose hips can be gathered wherever wild roses grow. Harvest the small fruits as soon as they become ripe in late summer. Dry them quickly, since they tend to split and become wormy.

Brewing: Rose hips have a long history as a brewing adjunct and are still used today as a key ingredient in some commercial beers from Poland. They impart a citrusy flavor and a red color to beer. Use ¼ to 1 ounce (7 to 28 g) of rose hips late in the boil.

Rosemary

Rosmarinus officinalis

Family: Labiatae (Mint)

Description: Woody, evergreen shrub with scaly bark and grayish green needles. Bears ½-inch (1.2 cm), pale blue flowers in late winter or spring. In northern areas, it may not bloom at all. Attractive to bees.

Similar species: None

Hardiness: Zones 8 to 10. Gardeners in cooler regions may overwinter plants inside on windowsills, but it's not always successful. Potted plants need to go through a reverse "hardening off" process before being taken inside for winter. Bring pots indoors to a south-facing window in a cool room for an increasing amount of time to help the plants adapt to the new environment.

Best site: Dry, slightly acidic, sandy soil with a pH of 6.0 to 6.5. Full sun to partial shade. Plants prefer a cool, moist climate. Will not survive if overwatered, but should be watered occasionally.

Propagation: Cuttings or divsion work best. Seeds germinate unevenly, and the young seedlings don't always survive.

Harvesting: Leaves can be cut throughout the season. Harvest no more than 20 percent of the total growth at one time.

Brewing: Rosemary was an essential part of the "ale grout" — a brewer's bouquet of herbs used to flavor ale in Europe before the introduction of hops. Use 1½ ounces (42 g) of fresh leaves late in the boil for flavor and aroma. Or use for dry hopping in fermenter to add a stronger piney scent to your beer.

Sage

Salvia officinalis

Garden sage

Family: Labiatae (Mint)

Description: Woody perennial with wiry
stems and oblong, gray-green, puck-
ered leaves. Bears spikes of white to
purple-blue flowers in early summer.
Attractive to bees. Grows 12 to
30 inches (30–75 cm) tall.

Similar species: See Clary Sage
(page 72)

Hardiness: Zones 4 to 8. In areas with cold
winters and unreliable snow cover, sage
should be mulched during winter.

Best site: Well-drained, moderately rich, slightly acidic soil (pH
6.2–6.4). Full sun. It will thrive in a heavy, moist soil, but probably won't survive a northern winter in such a location.

Propagation: Division and cuttings work well. Seeds can be sown
½ inch (1 cm) deep in soil in spring, either indoors or where the
plants are to stand.

Harvesting: Leaves should be picked before the flowers bloom in
early summer. Sage is best picked in the afternoon when the
plant's essential oils peak in strength.

Brewing: Sage has a history as a brewing ingredient dating back
to fifteenth-century English recipes. Add ½ ounce (14 g) of
fresh leaves midway through the boil to add some bitterness
and a camphorlike scent. The leaves can also be put directly into
the fermenter.

Savory

Satureja hortensis

Summer Savory

Family: Labiatae (Mint)

Description: Summer savory is a
hardy annual growing to 1½ feet
(.5 m) high, with small, lance-shaped
leaves. It bears small, white to lavender
blossoms from about 90 days after
planting until frost.

Similar species: Winter savory *(S. montana)* is a
fairly hardy perennial (zones 5 to 9), that grows
from 1½ to 2 feet (45 to 60 cm) tall. The leaves are thicker and
shinier than summer savory. It blooms from midsummer to frost
and is best propagated by root cuttings. This plant prefers a light,
alkaline, well-drained soil. Although the flavor is not as strong,
winter savory is generally interchangeable with summer savory as
a brewing ingredient.

Hardiness: Hardy annual

Best site: A rich, sandy soil with even moisture and full sun. Soil pH
should be between 6.5 and 7.5.

Propagation: Seeds germinate well.

Harvesting: The top 4 inches (10 cm) of a branch with flowers
should be cut as the flowers come into bloom.

Brewing: Use 1 ounce (28 g) of the flowers and leaves late in the boil
for a peppery, oregano-like flavor and aroma. The same amount
can also be added to a secondary fermenter for a more distinct
spicy aroma.

Spruce

Picea spp.

Colorado blue spruce *(P. pungens)*, Norway spruce *(P. abies)*, white spruce *(P. glauca)*

Family: Pinaceae (Pine)

Description: Colorado blue spruce (illustrated): evergreen tree 40 to 50 feet (12 to 15 m) tall with sharp, stout, gray-green to bright blue foliage. Prone to aphids. Norway spruce: evergreen tree 60 to 90 feet (18 to 27 m) tall with drooping, smooth, blue-green foliage. White spruce: evergreen tree 50 to 60 feet (15 to 18 m) tall with blue-green, smooth foliage.

Hardiness: Zones 3 to 6

Best site: As a group, spruces tolerate a wide range of conditions. They will grow in almost any soil, from dry to boggy, or any light, from full sun to full shade. Spruces prefer a climate with cold winters.

Propagation: Spruces can be grown from seeds or grafting, but it's much easier, and more common, to buy young balled-and-burlapped or container-grown saplings. Plant these trees in a hole amended with a bit of organic matter — but don't make the soil too rich or the tree's roots won't spread beyond the hole into the ground. Water well during the first season. Fertilize with compost or manure in the fall.

Harvesting: You can collect the branch tips throughout the season. New growth works the best for brewing; cut young branch tips when they are several inches long and pliable.

Brewing: Spruce beer gained popularity among colonial troops during the American Revolution. Use ¼ to 4 ounces (7 to 113 g) of fresh spruce tips late in the boil for a distinct, sweet woodsy taste and aroma.

Sweet Woodruff   *Galium odoratum*

Woodruff, Waldmeister

Family: Rubiaceae (Madder)

Description: Fragrant perennial ground-
cover with radiating clusters of pea
green leaves. Grows to 8 inches (20 cm)
tall. Bears small white flowers in May
and June.

Similar species: None

Hardiness: Zones 4 to 8

Best site: Moist, well-drained, acidic soil
enriched with compost, leaf mold, or other
organic matter. It requires partial to full shade
and prefers to be under trees.

Propagation: Division or cuttings of the underground rhizomes
(rootlike stems) works best. Sweet woodruff will sprout from
seeds, but only if they are fresh. Germination is slow.

Harvesting: Pick the leaves throughout the season. Dry the leaves
before using, since the herb has no scent when fresh but acquires
a strong, pleasant aroma as it dries.

Brewing: Sweet woodruff is native to the beech forests of Europe,
where it was first used as a brewing and winemaking ingredient.
The leaves are traditionally used in Berliner Weissbier and are also
dry hopped in white wine to make Maibowle or May wine.
Steeping ¼ ounce (7 g) of the dried leaves in a secondary fermenter for a few days before bottling should add a mild, sweet,
woodsy aroma with hints of vanilla to your beer.

Thyme

Thymus vulgaris

Common thyme, gardenthyme

Family: Labiatae (Mint)

Description: Small shrubs with tiny, dark green leaves. Grows up to 1 foot (.3 m) tall. Bears many s mall pink to lilac flowers in mid-summer. Attractive to bees. Distinctive flavor and scent.

Similar species: Creeping thyme *(T. serpyllum)* is a purple-flowered, low-growing ground cover. Lemon thyme *(T. x citriodorus)* is a small lemon-scented bush 6 to 8 inches (15 to 20 cm) tall.

Hardiness: Zones 4 to 9. In areas with cold winters, thyme should be covered with plenty of mulch for winter protection.

Best site: Poor, dry, well-drained, limey soil. Full sun to partial shade.

Propagation: Cuttings, division, or seeds will work.

Harvesting: Pick the leaves before the plants come into bloom in early summer.

Brewing: It seems as though the brewers of Mumm in the fifteenth century were willing to toss any herb with a strong smell into the brew kettle or fermenting barrel — thyme was no exception. Use ½ ounce (14 g) of fresh stems and leaves late in the boil to add a distinctive spicy taste and aroma. The same amount can also be added to the fermenter for a stronger scent.

Valerian

Valeriana officinalis

Garden heliotrope, cat's valerian, Greek valerian

Family: Valarianaceae (Valerian)

Description: A vigorous, spreading perennial with fernlike leaves that cluster at the base of the plant. Bears clusters of fragrant, pinkish white flowers during summer. Grows up to 4 feet (1.2 m) tall.

Similar species: Valerian has been recognized as safe by the United States Food and Drug Administration. It should not be confused with red valerian *(Centranthus ruber),* an ornamental plant that should not be used in brewing.

Hardiness: Zones 4 to 9

Best site: Prefers a rich, moist loam. Full sun to partial shade.

Propagation: Division in spring or fall. Valerian seeds have a short shelf life and ideally should be planted as soon as they ripen. Germination of spring-planted valerian is enhanced by cold treatment. Sow the seeds ¼ inch (.6 cm) deep, seal the pot in a freezer bag, and put it in the refrigerator or a cold outbuilding for three days. Bring the pot back inside to a warm spot to germinate. Transplant the seedlings out as early in spring as the soil can be worked.

Harvesting: Pick the leaves and flowers as soon as the plants come into bloom. Roots can be dug up when the plant is at least two years old.

Brewing: German brewers started adding valerian roots to their herbal ales in the fifteenth century. The herb has a mild sedative quality like that of hops; the roots are stronger than the leaves and flowers. Use ½ ounce (14 g) of fresh leaves and flowers late in the boil. Or add ¼ to ½ ounce (7 to 14 g) of dried root to your fermenter for a soothing flavor and pleasant scent.

Wintergreen

Gaultheria procumbens

Teaberry, Spiceberry, Mountain Tea, Boxberry

Family: Ericaceae (Heath)

Description: A vigorous, creeping, evergreen shrub growing to a height of 4 inches (10 cm) with woody stems and glossy, oval leaves. It bears insignificant flowers in summer followed by bright red berries in fall. Often grows wild in infertile evergreen forests.

Similar species: None

Hardiness: Zones 3 to 8

Best site: Rich, well-drained, acidic soil with a pH range of 4.5 to 5.5. Can handle full sun to full shade but prefers afternoon shade if possible.

Propagation: Seeds, nursery stock, or stem cuttings should be planted in the fall.

Harvesting: Pick the leaves throughout the season.

Brewing: Wintergreen leaves are used in brewing exactly like black birch twigs, but the flavor of black birch is superior. While the leaves have very little flavor, especially when dried, wintergreen's cooling aroma adds a nice touch to many beers. Use ¼ to 2 ounces (7 to 57 g) of fresh leaves late in the boil or in the secondary fermenter.

Yarrow
Achillea millefolium
Milfoil, devil's nettle

Family: Compositae (Daisy)

Description: Fern-leaved, spreading
perennial that grows up to 3 feet
(.9 m) tall. Bears clusters of white
to yellow flowers throughout summer.
Good dried flower. Many hybrids
available with different colored flowers, such as 'Summer Pastels.'
Widespread roadside weed, easily
gathered from the wild.

Similar species: Fern-leaf yarrow *(A. filipendulina)*
has large flowers and grows 3 feet (.9 m) tall; cultivars include
'Coronation Gold', 'Parker's Variety'.

Hardiness: Zones 3 to 8

Best site: Will grow in most soils, but prefers mildly acid soil with a
pH around 6. Full sun.

Propagation: Propagation is by seed or division in spring or fall.
Yarrow clumps should be divided every three to four years to
keep them vigorous.

Harvesting: Pick leaves and flowers soon after the plants come
into bloom.

Brewing: Yarrows leaves and blossoms were widely used to bitter
beer before hops became popular. Use ½ ounce (14 g) of fresh
leaves or blossoms early in the boil for a mild, sagelike bittering
to your beer.

THE NAMING OF PLANTS

You'll have noticed that we include a lot of names for herbs, both common and botanical. We've done that for a very simple reason: to make them easier to find. Some people call a plant by one of its names, others use another. Plants go by different common names in different parts of the United States, not to mention the rest of the world.

Botanical names are designed to be universal. Even though the taxonomists change them from time to time, essentially they are. All over the world, whatever language is being spoken, *Humulus lupulus* means hops.

If you go to a nursery and can't find a plant under one name, try another. It's said that no one uses botanical names, but you'll find most horticultural professionals know them and can point you in the right direction.

Seed catalogs are another place where a little Latin comes in handy. Very few seed catalogs use no botanical names. A few use only botanical names. Most have them listed somewhere, and it's a good idea to look at them before you order. Especially since betony is a brewing herb, while woolly betony is not — and you're likely to find both listed under lamb's-ears.

Homegrown Grains and Homemade Malts

GROWING some of your own grains for homebrewing will seem excessive to some people, but it's really not that complicated. A standard garden-sized plot of 800 square feet (74 m²) can easily produce enough barley in one year for five full all-grain, 5-gallon (19 L) batches. It can produce enough for at least 30 homebrew batches if you use a partial-mash recipe. Growing, harvesting, threshing, and malting your own grains for beer requires an extra investment of time and a willingness to work with nature. But you will truly put the "home" into your home-brewing and end up improving the control of final quality you have over your beers.

Unless you have a farm, it's unlikely that you can grow all the grains you'll need for all your brewing. We suggest that you start out by growing small crops of different kinds of grains. Any good-sized garden has room for at least a couple of rows of amaranth or corn, both of which are multipurpose plants. If you don't want to brew with them, you can always eat them. You can also experiment by planting some rows of barley to harvest later for making a single batch of specialty malt. And even if you don't want to grow your own, you can always buy unmalted grain from some local farmer or feed store and malt it yourself using the techniques we will describe.

The greatest advantage of home-malting (whether or not you grow the grain yourself) — beyond the simple satisfaction of the act — is that you can bring the cost of brewing a batch of beer down to almost nothing. Unmalted grain costs pennies a pound. With a little work you can transform the humble material into the finest, freshest beermaking malt available.

Barley *(Hordeum vulgare)*

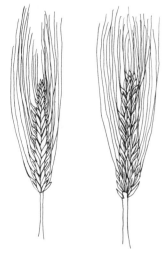

2-row barley   6-row barley

Barley is the king of all beer-making grains. It is one of the oldest and most useful of all cultivated plants. It has been around at least since Neolithic times. Most barley is now used for animal feed. Up to a third grown in the United States is for malting, mostly bearded six-row varieties in the upper Midwest and two-row varieties grown in the Pacific Northwest and Great Plains regions. The terms "6-row" and "2-row" refer to the number of rows of seeds on the spike of the seedhead. The 2-row has grains growing in a single row on either side of the head; 6-row has rows of grain all around the head.

Malting 6-row barley produces less extract than malting 2-row, but 6-row barley has plenty of enzymes to help convert starches to sugars. That makes it very useful in brewing beers that use unmalted adjuncts. The larger, starchier kernel and thinner hull of 2-row barley results in lots of extract and fewer off-flavors from hull tannins. It prefers milder climates than 6-row varieties. American 2-row varieties are somewhat more enzymatic than British versions. Another advantage of 2-row over 6-row barleys is that 2-row varieties are more prone to tillering, which is putting out extra side shoots. Since each of these extra stalks can produce another head, tillering can greatly improve yields. In a good year a barley plant may produce three or four tillers, in a poor year only one or two.

Culture

Barley is a very easy crop to cultivate compared with some of the other brewing grains. For this reason alone it recommends itself to the home grower. It can be planted in late spring, because its short growing season allows it to reach maturity in a hurry. Barley can be grown in a wide variety of soils and rainfall levels and does well in most of North America. Some varieties suffer from "lodging," a tendency to fall over and clump from wind and rain.

Varieties

Malting barleys have been specially bred over time to make good beer. There are many traditional cultivars still being grown, and new improved varieties are appearing every year in response to the needs of commercial growers. Some of these new types may suit your soil and conditions. Or you can stick with the old favorites, which were selected by small growers over thousands of years to make the very best beer.

The difference between "hulled" and "hulless" barley is really just one of degree. Old-fashioned hulled barley has a thick outer husk; newer varieties, such as Easy-Thresh Hulless, have been bred to have a thinner skin.

▸ CDC Stratus

Days to maturity, 90; 2-row; large, plump kernels; very productive, high-yielding grain; disease and drought resistent; short stalks 1½ feet (45 cm) high; low lodging; easy to thresh. New strain from Canada that outperforms 'Harrington'.

▸ Harrington

Days to maturity, 90; two-row; very productive but difficult to thresh by hand. Grows 2 feet (60 cm) tall.

▸ Easy-Thresh Hulless

Days to maturity, 90; 2-row; large heads; very productive, some lodging. Grows 3 feet (90 cm) tall. Easy to thresh. Has succeeded in home garden trials in Texas. Makes excellent malt.

▸ Excelsior

Days to maturity, 90; 6-row, large heads, purple seeds; vigorous, productive, little lodging. Easily hand-threshed. Grows 40 inches (102 cm) tall. Has performed well in home garden trials in Maine.

▸ 2-row Klages

Days to maturity, 90; 2-row. A very good malting variety widely grown in the United States.

Seed Sources

The only commercial catalog source for specific barley cultivars we've found is Grain Exchange/Garden Grains (see appendix B). It offers seeds of staple grains in quantities suited to garden-scale brewing patches, including wheat, rye, hulless oats, hulless barley, corn, amaranth, and many rare or heirloom cultivars.

The Grain Exchange also maintains a members-only cultivar exchange along the lines of the Seed Savers Exchange.

Homebrew supply shops and natural food stores, your Cooperative Extension Service, state farm bureaus, feed and seed stores, local organic farming organizations, and online sources such as university agricultural programs are all good places to start looking. There are a number of big seed companies online, but most don't accept small orders. If you live in a barley-producing region, try to track down a farmer who is growing malting barley, which has been specially bred to make beer. If you can't find any other source, try ordering unmalted barley through a homebrew store.

As a last resort, most of the barley you find in the bin at a health food store is likely to be 2-row malting barley. We've tried this and it works. Sprout a few in a jar and compare it with the malts you are used to using. If it's not too old, it will probably sprout for you. If you want to know whether it's worth brewing with, malt a batch and use it. The experiment won't cost you much time or money. If the malt is acceptable, try sowing a patch in the early spring. In eighty or ninety days you will have a harvest and will know for sure whether your grain is 2-row or 6-row. Granted this is a pretty random way to go about getting barley seed, but if you have no other sources it can work fine. Also, you may be able to find out where the store gets its barley and backtrack to ask the variety. If the seed is grown in the United States, there's a high probability that it will be 2-row Klages, a very good malting variety.

Once you have your seeds, you won't need to buy again. Just save a small percentage of your harvest for next year's sowing.

Expected Yield

A plot of ground measuring just 20 x 40 feet (6 x 12 m) will produce a bushel of barley in one planting. Since a bushel weighs approximately 47 pounds (21 kg), one crop of barley on an average garden plot can produce the grain ingredients for up to five batches of all-grain beer, or thirty or more batches of extract or partial mash. On a smaller scale, if grown intensively in good garden soil in raised beds with frequent waterings and good sun, a grower can expect roughly 5 to 15 pounds (2.3 to 6.8 kg) of grain per 10 x 10 foot (3 x 3 m) bed.

Soil Preparation

Barley grown for malt needs plenty of phosphorus, lime (calcium), and potassium in the soil, but not too much nitrogen. Barley tolerates slightly alkaline soil, but it dislikes acidic soil. A neutral soil pH suits it best. The optimum level depends in part on the kind of soil you have. The University of Delaware Cooperative Extension Service recommends that for light (sandy) soils maintain a pH from 5.8 to 6.0. For medium soils, the pH should be 6.0 to 6.2. And for heavy (clay) soils, a pH of 6.2 to 6.5 is recommended. The land does not have to be as fertile as it does for other grain crops such as wheat. Amending the soil with composted manure (make sure it's composted, or it will contain too much nitrogen); lime (only if soil tests show pH is acidic); rock phosphate for phosphorus; and greensand, granite dust, or wood ashes for potassium will provide all the nutrients your barley will need.

Planting and Care

Barley should be planted in very dry soil to grow well, which usually means that you have to wait a while for the ground to dry out in the spring. The simplest method of planting barley is broadcasting, which simply means spreading seeds evenly over the ground. Scatter the seeds fairly thickly over soil that has been raked smooth. For an 800-square-foot (74 m²) garden you need 5 to 7 pounds (2.3 to 3 kg) of seeds. Then rake the seeds into the surface soil and water lightly to ensure good contact between the seeds and soil.

PLANTING TIMES

You can plant barley outside in either spring or fall, or both, depending on your climate. Winterkill will affect barley in areas that average below 20°F (-6°C).

Once you've planted your barley, you won't have much to worry about until harvest time. Maintain even moisture in the grain beds during the growing season. If you live in an area with abundant early rainfall, you may not have to water at all. Quit watering when the plants start to turn from green to gold in late summer, to allow the heads to mature and dry.

Harvesting

When the grain is ready to harvest, the stalks should be golden; the individual grains should be hardening and difficult to dent with a fingernail, but not brittle. They will have lost about 30 percent of their water content at this point. The ears will be bent over. The grains will be pale yellow and hard and will easily pull off the head. The straw will be dry. Wait until the grains are perfectly mature before cutting the stalks.

The cut stalks then need to dry. You can leave the stalks lying in the field for about one week until they are completely dry. If

STARTING BARLEY INDOORS

When growing barley or any other grain on a very small scale, consider starting your seeds indoors, as you would any other garden vegetable. This is a good idea for people who have limited space and want to make the most of it. Start barley in seed trays or six-pack cell blocks in a soil-less mix. Plan on about 500 or 600 plants for a 100-square-foot (9.3 m²) plot. Malting barley has been bred to sprout well, so you should get good germination. Transplant the seedlings, being very careful of the roots, when they are an inch (2.5 cm) tall, about one week after emergence. Space them 5 inches (13 cm) apart in all directions.

CUTTING TOOLS

The barley can be cut down with a scythe or a string trimmer, or even with a pair of garden shears if you've got nothing else. A sharp hand sickle is probably the best tool for a small plot. For anything much larger, consider buying a European-style scythe such as the one offered by Fedco (see appendix B). This has a light, hand-forged head and sells for about 100 dollars. The traditional American scythe is a backbreaker, good for weed whacking and not much else. The European scythe is lighter and easier to work with. When using either a scythe or sickle, don't just swing wildly at the plants. Measured swings and a very sharp tool are all you need. With the sickle, you grasp a handful of stalks and cut with an easy motion. With the scythe, both hands are on the tool; the mower swings the blade easily from right to left, walking forward and keeping the base of the blade close to the ground. The blade needs to be sharpened at the end of each row to maintain razor sharpness.

rain is in the forecast, collect the stalks and cover them with a tarp. You can also collect the stalks in small bundles about 6 inches (15 cm) in diameter. To help the drying process, stack six or more of these bundles (also called sheaths) together. Place the cut ends against the ground, and push the heads of the sheaths together so they intermesh and support each other. Make one extra-large sheath to put on top as a rain cover. After the stalks are dry, stack the grain loose until you're ready to thresh it.

Threshing and Winnowing

Threshing is the process of separating the grains from the dried seedheads. Lay out a large, clean dropcloth or piece of plastic sheeting on a hard, flat surface such as a garage floor. Take the barley two handfuls at a time, lay it on the dropcloth, and hit it with a plastic baseball bat, broom handle, or similar tool. Each bundle will produce about a cup of grain. Remove the threshed straw, which can be composted or used as mulch or animal food.

Carefully pick up the corners of the tarp to bring the grain together. Then pour the grain, chaff, and bits of straw into a bucket.

Another method of threshing is to simply take the dry barley sheaths and whack the grain heads against the inside of a 5-gallon pail until they all come off.

Winnowing is the process of separating the grains from the bits of straw. Winnow the grain by pouring it carefully from one bucket to another, outside, with either a light breeze or a fan blowing to carry away the debris. The heavy grain should fall straight into the second bucket. Winnowing won't get the grain completely clean, but it will be clean enough as grain needs to be thoroughly rinsed as part of the malting process to come later.

OUTSIDE SOURCES FOR BARLEY AND OTHER GRAINS

You don't have to grow all of your own grains to make beer. There are plenty of other sources of grain ready for home malting.

Grains used in beermaking obviously have to be fit for human consumption, but that isn't as clear-cut as you might think. You don't want to use seed grain, because it may have been treated with some kind of chemical. Feed grain can be used, but there's a possibility that it may have been milled in some way, and it might not sprout. It might also contain weed seeds; while these probably won't hurt you, they won't improve the quality of your beer, either. The best option for most people, though it may be more expensive, is to get your unmalted grains from a homebrew store or catalog, health food store, or food co-op.

On the other hand, there are now a surprising number of organic growers producing brewing grain crops, even such odd varieties as spelt. You may be able to buy grain in quantity directly from some local farmer, which would certainly be a cheaper alternative. Get in touch with your local organic growers association, which can help you locate a source.

Storing the Barley

Since malting should be done in the cold temperatures of winter, you will need to store your barley for a time. The best way to do this is to place it in burlap sacks in a cool, but not damp, cellar. The grain will be able to breathe through the burlap. Barley will keep this way for several years.

Basic Barley Malting

Barley malting is best done in late fall or winter, when temperatures are cold. The temperature of your malting area should be around 50°F (10°C), if not cooler. There are two reasons for this, both having to do with the final quality of the malt. Warm temperatures cause germinating barley to bolt, or grow very rapidly into a green shoot. Warm temperatures also encourage molds, mildews, and fungi that can grow on wet grain.

Malting Instructions

To malt barley you'll need some basic equipment. Some of the items on the list are handy but optional; others are vital. This basic malting procedure is for 5 pounds (2.3 kg) of barley grain.

Two 5-gallon (19 L) plastic buckets

One 5-gallon (19 L) plastic bucket with ¹/₈-inch holes drilled in the bottom

Close-fitting (but not airtight) lid for the plastic bucket with holes

Large metal or plastic spoon

Thermometer: To take the temperature of the steeping water, germinating mass, etc.

Notebook: For recording your malting procedure, how long you steeped the grain, how long the grain took to germinate, any problems you encountered, etc.

20-pound (10 kg) scale (optional): To tell how much malt you have.

Aquarium pump with air stone (optional): Many homes have one of these somewhere, whether or not they currently keep fish. Buy a new air stone and hose for malting; don't just reuse an old one. Algae and fish waste don't mix with beer.

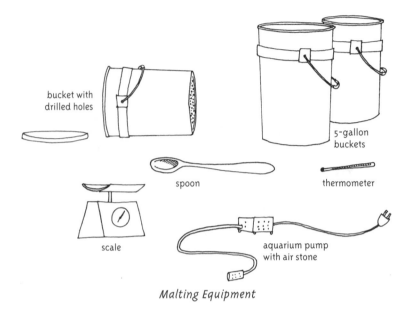

Malting Equipment

▸ Cleaning the grain

Before you clean the grain, weigh it. You'll need to know the dry weight in order to tell when the malted grain is dry (see page 120). Barley often contains bits of stem, chaff, weed seeds, and other debris that should be removed before malting. Most of this will float away if the grain is submerged in water; the heavier grain will sink. Pour the grain into one of the 5-gallon (19 L) plastic buckets and fill with water. Stir the grain and allow it to settle to the bottom. Skim off the debris with the spoon and put it in another container to compost or otherwise dispose of later. Don't just let it go down the sink; straw and germinating weed seeds can clog your pipes.

▸ Steeping the grain.

Steep the grain for a total of 72 hours in one of the plastic buckets. Cover grain with at least ½ gallon (2 L) of water

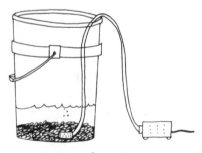

Steeping the grain

at 50°F (10°C). The steep
water should be changed after
2 hours, and every twelve
hours thereafter. Set the per-
forated plastic bucket (the
sieve bucket) firmly inside the
remaining (empty) plastic
bucket. Pour the grain and
water into the sieve bucket,
allowing the water to drain
completely. Return grain to
first bucket and cover with
fresh water.

Draining the grain

If an aquarium pump and air stone are used to aerate the steep
water, the water only needs to be changed once every 24 hours.
Put the air stone at the bottom of the bucket, among the grain.

After the steep, the grain will be soft and swollen. It will have
expanded to roughly 150 percent of its original volume.

▸ Germination

Drain the grain thoroughly
in the sieve bucket. The germination process should take
place in a dark room at about
50°F (10°C). The temperature
of the germinating mass should
be 59 to 65°F (12 to 15°C). It
shouldn't exceed 68°F (20°C).

Germination is much easier
to control if the aquarium
pump is used. First pour about
a gallon of water into the
5-gallon (19 L) bucket. Then
put the air stone into the

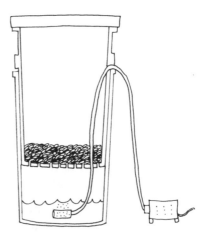

Germinating grain

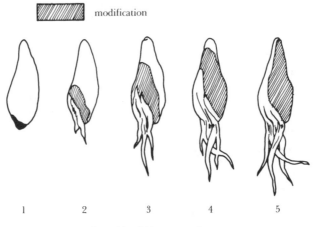

Growth of the acrospire

water and set the sieve bucket into the plastic bucket. Be careful not to crush the air hose. This arrangement will prevent the grain from drying out, scrub out carbon dioxide (which can suffocate the grain), and prevent heat buildup inside the mass. If this germinator setup is not used, the grain must be turned frequently.

After about three days of germination, rootlets will have begun to grow and the *acrospire,* or shoot, should be visible as a bulge under the husk.

Cutting open a grain of barley will tell you how far along the germination process has come. Once the acrospire has grown to two-thirds the length of the grain, it should be *couched*.

▸ Couching the malt

The next step in malting is couching. This process is basically a carbon dioxide bath that prevents the acrospire from growing (by denying it oxygen), yet allows enzymes to fully convert the grain starches into fermentable sugars. If you've been using the germinator setup described above, shut it off and seal the sieve bucket with the lid.

It's important to turn the germinating mass once a day, to prevent heat and carbon dioxide buildup from killing the grain. Grain should be couched for one to three days. Check the grain periodically to see if the acrospire is still growing. It shouldn't be. If it is, stop couching and kiln the malt.

▸ Kilning

Kilning, or drying the malt, presents its own problems. Grain can always be kilned in an oven; however, few ovens can maintain the kind of exacting control you'll need to produce usable pale malt for all-grain mashing. Commercial food dehydrators can give you this control, but they generally don't hold enough grain to make them worth bothering with.

If it's your intention to produce malt for all-grain mashing, you should build your own dryer, which will give you both volume and control. Instructions for building such a dryer can be found in the "1985 Special Grain Brewing Issue" of *Zymurgy* (Volume 8, number 4, 1985). An oast, such as the one described on page 38, might possibly be used to dry grain. However, we don't recommend using the same oast to dry both malt and hops — you'll get hop smell all through your malt, or malt smell all through your hops. One solution might be to build one bin just for malts. Make sure the mesh of the screen is small enough so that the grains don't fall through.

If all you want to do is produce your own specialty dark malts, the lowest setting on your oven should be sufficient. Spread the grain out on a baking sheet and dry it, stirring occasionally. To allow for air circulation, the door should be left slightly ajar. It should take about 48 hours to dry 5 pounds (2.3 kg) of wet malt.

Some experts recommend drying small amounts of malt tied in a pillowcase in the clothes dryer. It sounds elegant and simple. Unfortunately, it doesn't work, and it makes a mess of the dryer.

You can tell when the malt is dry when it weighs its original amount before the steeping process began.

▸ Roasting

Once the malt has been dried, it can be roasted in a regular oven to produce many specialty malts such as crystal malt. To produce a uniform product, malts should be spread no thicker than ¾ inch (2 cm) on a baking sheet. All home-roasted grains should be allowed to cool after roasting and stored in a cool, dry place to mellow for five to seven days before brewing.

• **Toasted malt.** Roast the dry, kilned malt at 350°F (178°C) for 10 to 15 minutes, until it is golden and aromatic.

• **Munich malt.** Roast dry, kilned malt at 350°F (178°C) for 20 minutes until lightly toasted.

• **Crystal malt.** Start with malt that is still wet, or "green." (Pale barley malt that has been soaked for 24 hours in cold water can be substituted for homemade malt.) Kiln it at the lowest setting until it is nearly dry. Raise the oven temperature to 200°F (93°C) and roast for 1 hour. Then raise the oven temperature to 350°F (178°C) and roast until the malt is dry and a golden brown color. This should take about 1½ to 2 hours.

• **Vienna malt.** Start with dry, kilned malt. Roast between 215 to 225°F (102 to 107°C) for 3 hours.

• **Roasted barley.** Start with clean, dry, unmalted barley. Roast it at 400°F (200°C) until it's a deep brown color, about 1 hour and 10 minutes.

• **Black patent malt.** Start with dry, finished malt. Spread the malt very thinly and roast at 350°F (178°C) for 1 hour and 20 minutes. Stir often to prevent burning. A certain amount of smoke in the kitchen is inevitable during this procedure.

• **Smoked malt.** Start with green (wet, finished but unkilned) malt. (Pale barley malt that has been soaked for 24 hours in cold water can be substituted for homemade malt.) Kiln it at the lowest setting until it is half dry. Sprinkle lightly with water and set aside for 12 hours. Soak mesquite, apple, or hickory wood chips overnight in water. You can experiment with different woods — each will impart a different character to your grains. Prepare a bed of coals in a traditional barbecue grill, or start a gas grill and set to low/medium. Drain the chips and place them in an even layer over the heat. Place the grains on a clean, fine-mesh screen over the fire. Cover the grill (leave the vents open) to get the full benefit of the smoke. Stir the grain every 5 minutes to prevent burning. Smoke the grain anywhere from 15 to 40 minutes until fully dry.

Other Grains

Barley is the most common grain used for brewing, but many other grains await the more adventurous homebrewer. Growing unusual grains can broaden your experience as a brewer as well as a gardener.

Amaranth (*Amaranthus* spp.)

Amaranth is an ancient grain that is enjoying a recent surge in popularity. Revered by the Aztecs, Incas, and Mayas in pre-Columbian times, amaranth is a tough, hardy, productive grain that requires almost no cultivation. Homebrewers in increasing numbers are now rediscovering the nutty flavors it contributes to beer. If allowed to, amaranth will self-sow, coming back every year in unexpected places with no help from you. It's a huge and dramatically beautiful plant, growing anywhere from 4 to 10 feet (1.2 to 3 m) tall. It bears large, complicated seed-heads, in any color from bronze to burgundy, above masses of edible leaves. Seeds are available from many mail-order gardening catalogs.

Varieties

▸ Burgundy (or Burgundy Elite)

Days to maturity, 90–120; productive variety. Small, white seeds. Grows 5 to 8 feet (1.5 to 2.4 m) tall with brilliant red foliage and drooping, red seedheads.

▸ Golden

Days to maturity, 90–95; short-season, productive to very productive strain. White seeds. Grows 6 to 9 feet (1.8 to 2.7 m) tall with towering gold seedheads.

▸ Golden Giant

Days to maturity, 98–120; very productive, midseason variety. Yields up to 1 pound (.45 kg) per plant have been reported. White seeds. Grows 6 to 7 feet (1.8 to 2.1 m) tall with bronze-striped leaves and orange-gold seedheads.

▸ Opopeo

Days to maturity, 100; early-season variety for cold areas. White seeds. Over 7 feet (2.1 m) tall with maroon seedheads.

Planting and Care

Plant the seeds after all danger of frost has passed, when the soil has warmed. Amaranth isn't picky about soil, growing in anything from heavy clay to dust, but it must have full sun. Sow thickly in furrows ⅛ to ¼ inch (3 to 6 mm) deep. Space rows 18 inches (45 cm) apart. Water until the first true leaves appear, then thin the seedlings to stand 10 to 18 inches (25 to 45 cm) apart. The plants need very little water once the first leaves appear. They can survive without supplemental watering except in periods of extreme drought.

Harvesting

Large, pendulous seedheads form in mid- to late summer. The grain will ripen by early autumn. The seeds are ripe when they fall out of the seedheads easily if disturbed. In arid climates the seedheads can be left on the plants to dry completely. Otherwise, it's a good idea to cut off the seedheads and either allow them to dry out, or process them immediately and then dry the grain.

Threshing

Strip the florets with grain from each spike of the seedheads into a paper bag. Rub the chaff and grain through either a wire mesh frame or a large sieve into another container. The grain (and remaining chaff) can then either be put through a finer mesh or winnowed. Unless you have a really big harvest, we don't recommend winnowing; unless you're a skilled hand, too much grain gets lost to make it worthwhile.

Malting

Amaranth is very easy to malt using a simple technique. The grain has no hull, so it doesn't have to be soaked for a long time.

1. Soak the grain for 12 hours in a jar covered with cheesecloth. Drain and rinse the grain with cold water. Put it in a warm place out of direct sunlight. Rinse the grain at least three times a day.

2. Check the grain. On the third or fourth day, the acrospire, or shoot, will have developed. It appears as a white circle around the outside of the grain. The center of the seed will have turned dark, and there may also be a root growing from the seed. The grain is now ready to be kilned.

3. Drain the grain and spread it out on a baking sheet or other shallow pan. Dry it in the oven on its lowest setting for electric models, or with the pilot light on for gas. This should take 2 to 6 hours. A pound (.45 kg) of seed will yield about 6 ounces (171 g) of malt.

Corn (Zea mays)

Corn is a traditional adjunct in many major commercial beers. It has also been used for centuries by the Andean Indians as the main ingredient producing *chicha de jora,* a frothy beer consumed fresh (not bottled or carbonated but right out of the fermenting vat).

Varieties

There are of course thousands of varieties, cultivars, and hybrids of corn. Along with tomatoes, corn is possibly the single most hybridized garden crop in the world. If you decide that you want to grow your own corn to brew historical beers like the tart tasting South American chicha or other styles, here are a few interesting suggestions to get you started.

▸ Ashworth
Days to maturity, 60–85; early, cold-tolerant, open-pollinated sweet corn. Plants grow 4 to 5½ feet (1.2 to 1.5 m) tall with 6- to 7-inch (15 to 18 cm) ears of bright yellow kernels.

▸ Black Aztec
Days to maturity, 68–110; early to midseason, pre-Columbian sweet corn heirloom from Mexico. Plants grow 4 to 6 feet (1.2 to 1.8 m) tall with 7-inch (17 cm) ears of white kernels that mature to blue-black. Perfect for making blue cornmeal or chicha de jora beer.

▸ Bloody Butcher

Days to maturity, 100–120; mid- to late season sweet or dent heirloom corn. Plants grow 8 to 12 feet (2.4 to 3.7 m) tall and bear two to six ears per stalk. Ears have red and pink kernels, with an occasional white ear.

▸ Peruvian Morado

Days to maturity, 90–100; Mexican heirloom field corn, can be eaten as sweet corn when young. Plants grow 4 to 6 feet (1.2 to 1.8 m) tall and bear 2½- to 6-inch (6 to 15 cm) ears of dark violet kernels. Traditional chicha de jora beer variety, now grown only for brewing.

Planting and Care

Unlike most of the grains in this section, corn is a finicky, particular kind of crop. Plant seeds in rich, moist loam after all danger of frost is past and the soil has warmed to at least 65°F (18°C). Plant three to four seeds every 12 inches (30 cm), 1 inch (2.5 cm) deep, in blocks 30 inches (76 cm) apart. When the seedlings are 4 inches (10 cm) tall, thin to 1 plant per foot (30 cm).

Spacing is critical. If the plants are too close, their growth will be stunted; too far away and they won't be pollinated properly. Pollination is also important. You have to plant at least four rows of corn to ensure pollination. If the corn silks aren't pollinated, kernels can't form. Corn is pollinated by the wind, not insects, and different varieties planted closer than ¼ mile (400 meters) will crossbreed. This won't make a difference in brewing corn, but it will if the crop is to be eaten fresh.

PROTECTING CORN

Protect seeds against birds, seedlings against deer, and ripening ears against raccoons by using netting, fencing, scarecrows, or a combination of all three.

Harvesting and Cleaning

When the ears are swollen and the corn silk has turned brown, the corn can be picked for fresh eating. Check for ripeness by pulling away the husk and piercing a kernel with a thumbnail. If the sap is milky, it's ready to pick.

For brewing purposes, corn must be fully mature. Allow the ears to stay on the stalks until the husks turn brown. This may be after several frosts. Then bring the husked corn inside to finish drying in a moderately warm place away from sunlight. When the cobs and kernels are fully dry, remove the kernels by rubbing two cobs together, which will take the kernels off both. Larger harvests can be cleaned using a mechanical corn sheller. Any debris left among the kernels can be winnowed out.

Malting

Corn malt is indispensable for brewing some types of indigenous beer such as chicha de jora. You can buy imported Andean *jora* corn malt in some South American markets in the United States, but the price is very high.

Home-malted corn can be inexpensively and easily made. It's probably best to make your own for homebrewing.

As with the other types of malt, you should use untreated corn that's fit for eating rather than seed corn.

1. Soak the corn in cold water for 24 hours.

2. If using small amounts (1–4 pounds/.45–1.8 kg), transfer to a colander for germination. If using larger amounts, you may want to use the plastic sieve bucket described under barley malting.

CORN MALTING SHORTCUT

It's easy enough to obtain dried sweet yellow corn in season, and for your first experiments in malting that's what we suggest you do.

3. Spray the corn with water twice a day. Turn it over completely once a day to prevent mold from growing.

4. Germination should occur within two days, and within five days the sprouts should grow to about 2 inches (5 cm) long. Expect only about half of the corn to sprout. The corn may develop a strong smell during germination; it's normal.

5. After germination is complete, the malted corn can be dried either in the sun on a plastic sheet, or in an oven. Use the lowest setting for electric ovens or dry with just the pilot light on for gas ovens.

6. When it is dry, malted corn can be stored indefinitely in a sealed container away from moisture.

Oat Malt

Oat beers were traditionally made from malted oats. This is no longer done commercially, if at all. Modern homebrewers and microbrewers rely on flaked or steel-cut oats. The reason for this is simple: Germinating oats tend to attract *butryfying bacteria*. The *butanol* isomers that these bacteria produce are poisonous, as are the microbes themselves. We consider oat malting a risky business and advise you not to try it.

Quinoa *(Chenopodium quinoa)*

Quinoa (pronounced "Keen-wah") is native to the Andes mountains of South America. Used as a staple grain by the Incas and Aztecs, its pungent qualities are being used by some homebrewers looking to add unique flavors to their beer. Quinoa is well adapted to growing at elevations above 8,000 feet (2,400 m). Often grown for its tangy leaves, quinoa resembles the weed lamb's-quarters, especially when young. Quinoa is very drought tolerant, but it needs cool nights in order to flower.

Varieties

Quinoa seeds of the following varieties are available from a number of mail-order gardening catalogs.

▸ Dave (or # 407)

Days to maturity, 90–100; very short season, very productive variety adaptable to most elevations. Yellow-brown, small to medium-sized seeds. Plants grow 5 to 6 feet (1.5 to 1.8 m) tall with gold seedheads.

▸ Faro

Days to maturity, 100–130; drought-tolerant, fast-growing, very productive Chilean type. Adaptable to much of the United States. Small, white seeds. Grows 4 to 6 feet (1.2 to 1.8 m) tall.

▸ Isluga (or Isluga Yellow)

Days to maturity, 90–120; early maturing, high-yielding, adaptable Chilean variety. Medium-sized yellow seeds. Grows 5 to 7 feet (1.5 to 2.1 m) tall with beautiful yellow to pink seedheads.

▸ Multi-hued

Days to maturity, 100–120; amazingly productive midseason variety. Plants grow 5 to 7 feet (1.5 to 2.1 m) tall; they are sometimes broken by the weight of orange, red, yellow, purple, or mauve seedheads.

Planting and Care

Plant the seeds after all danger of frost has passed, when the soil has warmed to 55 to 60°F (12 to 15°C). Space seeds 4 to 6 inches (10 to 15 cm) apart, in rows 20 inches (51 cm) apart. Water only until the seedlings appear. Thin seedlings to stand 8 inches (20 cm) apart. The thinnings can be eaten. The plants are very drought tolerant, needing only 10 to 12 inches (25 to

30 cm) of water per season to produce grain. Seedheads similar to those of amaranth form in midsummer.

Harvesting

The grain should be harvested after the first frost of autumn. Allow the plants to dry out for a few days before cutting the seedheads. Quinoa plants show some resistance to light frost, which won't hurt the mature grain. Hang the seedheads in a dark, dry place with good air circulation to completely dry. In humid climates, you may need to thresh the grain (see page 123) while the heads are still moist, then dry it completely to prevent molding.

Malting

Quinoa grain is covered with a natural soapy substance (saponin) that should be washed off before the grain is brewed with or cooked. Quinoa can be added either malted or unmalted to beer. It's a small, round grain without a hull, very similar in structure to amaranth. It can be malted using the same procedures.

1. Soak the grain for 12 hours in a jar covered with cheese-cloth. Drain and rinse the grain with cold water. Put in a warm place out of direct sunlight. Rinse the grain at least three times a day.

2. Check the grain. On the third or fourth day, the acrospire, or shoot, will have grown. It appears as a white circle around the outside of the grain, and the center of the seed will have turned dark. There may also be a root growing from the seed. The grain is now ready to be kilned.

3. Drain the grain and spread it out on a baking sheet or other shallow pan. Dry it in the oven on its lowest setting for electric models, or with just the pilot light on for gas. This should take 2 to 6 hours. A pound (.45 kg) of seed will yield about 6 ounces (171 g) of malt.

Rye Malt

Rye malt has historically been used to make such beers as German roggenbier and Finnish sahti. However, rye has many of the same problems as oat malt, only to a much greater degree. If not handled properly, malting rye can also produce dangerous microbes. As a result, we advise you leave malting this grain to the professionals. Rye malt is gaining in popularity among homebrewers and microbrewers alike and is increasingly available commercially. Chances are your homebrew store stocks it. If not, they can special order it for you.

Sorghum (*Sorghum bicolor*)

Beer made with sorghum outsells Western-style beers seven to one in South Africa. In fact, Guinness adapted its famous stout recipe to include sorghum as an ingredient for the South African market. Sorghum's sweet taste is balanced with a refreshing tartness when used in brewing. It comes in four different types: grain, sweet, grass, and broomcorn. All will produce seeds, but only grain and sweet sorghums are suitable for brewing. Sweet sorghum is grown for its stalks, which are crushed and rendered down for their sweet sap. The sap is then boiled, much like maple syrup, to produce a thick syrup similar to molasses. Using sorghum syrup as a fermentable brewing adjunct may be the easiest option for the adventurous homebrewer.

Varieties

Sorghum seeds are available through several gardening catalogs as well as other sources.

▸ Mennonite
Days to maturity, 90–95; Early, productive sweet sorghum variety. Reddish seeds. Grows 7 to 10 feet (2.1 to 3 m) tall with large, orange-red seedheads.

▸ **White African**

Days to maturity, 100–120; midseason, very productive, fast-growing sweet sorghum. White seeds. Grows 10 to 12 feet (3 to 3.7 m) tall with very dramatic, black and white seedheads.

Planting and Care

Plant the seeds a week or so before the frost-free date (or indoors three to four weeks before the frost-free date). Space the seeds 7 inches (18 cm) apart in rows 2 to 3 feet (.6 to .9 m) apart. Water only until the seedlings appear. Thin seedlings to stand 14 inches (35 cm) apart. Sorghum plants are very heat and drought tolerant; they will thrive even in poor soil. In frost-free areas (zones 10 and 11) they may be perennial. Seedheads form in midsummer; the grain becomes ripe by late summer or early autumn.

Harvesting

The grain should be harvested when the plants begin to dry in early autumn. In humid climates, sorghum is prone to the same problems as amaranth and quinoa; it may have to be cut before it dries completely. The seedheads can be hung up to air-dry for a few days before cleaning. Cut the tassels off and rub the grain and chaff off between your hands. Compared to amaranth and quinoa, sorghum grains are fairly large and heavy, making it easy to winnow them (outside, either in a light breeze or in front of a fan) without losing grain.

Malting

1. Soak the sorghum in cold water for 18 hours. Drain it in the sieve bucket.

2. Leave the sorghum in the sieve bucket to germinate. Rinse it with cool water every 8 hours. Turn it occasionally to insure even germination. The sorghum should sprout in two or three days. When the acrospire is ¾ to 2 inches (1.9 to 5 cm) long, it's time to kiln the grain.

3. After germination is complete, the malted grain can be dried either in the sun on a plastic sheet, or in an oven. Drain and rinse the grain and spread it out on a baking sheet or other shallow pan. Dry it in the oven on its lowest setting for electric models, or with just the pilot light on for gas. Stir the grain occasionally. This should take 6 to 12 hours. The malted grain can be stored indefinitely in a sealed container away from moisture.

Spelt *(Triticum spelta)*

Spelt is an ancient form of wheat that can be malted to make a hypo-allergenic beer for people who are allergic to the gluten from ordinary wheat. Ale recipes using spelt date back to the seventeenth century in Holland.

Varieties

Spelt seeds are available through some of the mail-order garden catalogs listed in the back of the book.

▸ **Champ**

Days to maturity, 120; brown-chaffed cultivar that outyields common spelt by 23 percent. Strong stems. Resists leaf rust but is moderately susceptible to powdery mildew.

Planting and Care

Much like barley, spelt should be planted in very dry soil in the spring to grow well. Scatter the seeds fairly thickly over soil that has been raked smooth. Rake the seeds into the surface soil and water lightly. Spelt requires very little care once planted. The plants will grow rapidly. In late summer they'll be ready for harvest.

Harvesting

Cut down the stalks and let them dry out for one week. Lay the dry stalks on a sheet on a hard, flat surface and thresh (see page 113). Pick up the corners of the sheet and pour the grain into a bucket. Winnow to separate out the debris (see page 114). Store the resulting grain in burlap sacks in a cool, dry cellar until cool weather malting.

Malting

Spelt is malted much the same way as barley. Maintain cool (50–55°F/10–12°C) temperatures, and keep out of direct light.

1. Soak 5 pounds (2.3 kg) of spelt in cold, fresh water in the 5-gallon bucket for 24 hours. Drain it in the sieve bucket. Soak for 8 more hours and drain again.

2. Leave the spelt in the sieve bucket to germinate. Rinse it with cool water every 8 hours. Turn it occasionally to prevent molding. The spelt should sprout in 2 or 3 days. When the acrospire (sprout) is the same length as the grain, it's time to kiln.

3. Drain and rinse the grain and spread it out on a jelly-roll pan or other shallow pan. Dry it in the oven, using the lowest setting for electric models, or just the pilot light for gas. Stir the grain occasionally. This should take 6 to 12 hours. The dried grain should be crunchy and slightly sweet. It can be stored indefinitely in a sealed container away from moisture.

Wheat (Triticum aestivum)

Wheat can be grown the same way as barley, but it has several problems that make it difficult to malt. Wheat grains have no thick outer husk, which means the steeping process is much shorter. Also, the acrospire grows outside the grain, making the germinating mass difficult to turn. Finally, wheat malt must be kilned for many hours at 178°F (80°C). As a result, we recommend you simply use the wheat malt available commercially from most homebrew stores and catalogs.

Unmalted wheat is also often used for brewing. The flaked version of unmalted wheat is the easiest to use since it already is cooked — a necessary step before using it as a brewing ingredient. Unmalted wheat is added to lighten a beer's body and color. Unmalted wheat and other grains are available from many homebrew suppliers.

USING UNMALTED GRAINS

When brewing with any unmalted grains, including wheat and barley, remember that they always need to be used in combination with malted grains during mashing because unmalted grains lack the enzymes needed for starch conversion.

Beer Recipes

Using Homegrown Hops,
Brewing Herbs, and
Homemade Malts

THE beauty of having a garden is that no matter what you grow, you can probably use it as an adjunct in beer. You can probably even find a recipe for it somewhere. If it is an herb, fruit, or vegetable, it has most likely been used in beer at some point in time, so feel free to experiment. You may be the first person ever to brew cranberry-apple stout, but then again, maybe not.

For us, finding new combinations of ingredients, and new tastes, is one of the most satisfying aspects of homebrewing. We can never resist a new ingredient, or a new challenge.

Even if we aren't brewing an "herbal beer," we usually manage to slip a few homemade or homegrown ingredients into any beer we brew. Sometimes we just use home-cultured yeasts instead of the commercial varieties, a very economical step when you consider that a single packet of yeast may cost several dollars. Or we may include some wild-gathered Irish moss or spruce tips. But many of our beers are brewed with a large percentage of homemade ingredients. Because we make them from our own products, these beers are truly unique — no one else can make our brew quite the same way.

BREWING WITH THE REST OF THE GARDEN

If barley be wanting to make into malt
We must be content and think it no fault
For we can make liquor to sweeten our lips
Of pumpkins, and parsnips, and walnut-tree chips.

— Colonial American poem, 1630

Adding fruit and vegetables to beer is almost as old as brewing itself. Raspberries, blackberries, cherries, apricots, pears, kiwis, apples, pomegranates, and others are all worthy candidates for fruit beers. Vegetables such as pumpkins, squash, and chili peppers are popular beer flavorings. Other possibilities like potatoes, zucchini, parsnips, cucumbers, radishes, beets, carrots, turnips, eggplants, asparagus, Jerusalem artichokes, sweet peppers, burdock, cardoons, chicory, celeriac, arugula, horseradish, garlic, tomatoes, and sweet potatoes remain an almost unexplored frontier.

FRUIT

Fruit beers should either be very light in malt and hops, to allow the delicate flavors and aromas to come through, or very dark, to provide a malty counterpoint to the fruit flavors. Fruit beers should have only one-third the normal amount of bittering hops, and no flavoring or aroma hops to compete with the fruit. A good rule of thumb is to use 1 to 1½ pounds (.45 to .68 kg) of fruit per gallon (3.8 L) of beer. Fruit should not be boiled; it contains pectin, which can produce a hazy beer if boiled. Heat fruit just to 160°F (71°C), enough to kill any bacteria or wild yeasts that might otherwise threaten beer. One possibility is to add fruit to the brew pot after the boil and let the wort pasteurize the fruit, then ferment beer and fruit together. Allow the fruited beer to ferment for about six weeks, then rack it to a secondary fermenter, being careful to avoid siphoning up the fruit. The main disadvantage to this method is that in the furious activity of primary fermentation, the delicate fruit flavors and aromas will be driven off with carbon dioxide from the yeast. Another method avoids this problem, but requires advance planning. Brew your batch of potential fruit beer with only 4 gallons (15 L) of water. Allow it to undergo primary fermentation, then pasteurize the fruit in 1 gallon (4 L) of 160°F (71°C) water for 15 minutes. Cool the fruit "wort," transfer it to a secondary fermenter, and rack the unfinished beer onto it. Ferment the beer to completion and bottle it.

VEGETABLES

Vegetable beers are a bit trickier. Chili beers can be brewed using the same techniques as fruit beers, but if the chilies are used fresh, they should be roasted first. Wash the peppers, then roast them either on a grill or under a broiler until their skins blister and blacken. Put the chilies in either a bowl with a plate over it or a paper bag to steam until cool enough to handle, about 20 minutes. Remove the skin and seeds. Dried chilies can be added directly to the boil. Chilies should be used with care. The amount to use depends on the degree of heat desired in the finished beer, and the type of chili being used. Milder chilies can be used in larger amounts; Anaheims and New Mexico types can be used in amounts up to 1 pound (454 g). Hotter varieties should be used more sparingly.

Starchy vegetables such as squash, pumpkins, potatoes, parsnips, and the like need to be cooked first, to break down their starches into a form accessible to the enzymes of malt. Peel them and bake or boil until cooked. Add cooked vegetables to a simple infusion or step mash.

If a step mash is used, add vegetables during the second "step": mash in with 3 gallons (11 L) of 130°F (54°C) water. Stabilize at 122°F (50°C) and hold for 30 minutes. Add 1½ gallons (5.7 L) boiling water and vegetables. Stabilize at 148°F (64°C) and hold for 1 hour. Raise heat and mash-out at 165°F (68°C). Pumpkins and squash should be reduced to a pulp before mashing; potatoes should be kept as whole as possible to avoid a stuck runoff.

FLOWERS

The concept of brewing with flowers is a very old one. It is being explored again by modern homebrewers. Many of our brewing herbs are flowers; even hop cones are flowers, botanically speaking. Brewing herbs such as heather, hyssop, and lavender are small, tough blossoms that need a long boil to bring out their color and flavor in beer. Rose hips, although technically fruits, fall into this category. Another class of flowers for brewing is used to provide color and aroma, either in the brew pot after the boil, or dry hopped in the fermenter. These include nasturtiums, borage, chamomile, sweet woodruff, wild roses, scented geranium leaves, daylilies, marigolds, and calendula. Generally speaking, any flower that can be eaten can be added to beer.

MODIFYING RECIPES FOR HOMEGROWN INGREDIENTS

Remember that the ingredients you grow and make at home can have some different characteristics than store-bought ingredients because they are so much fresher.

▸ Hops — Homegrown hops tend to be much stronger than commercial ones due to freshness and the lack of processing. So a good rule when using your own hops is to tread lighter than you usually would.

▸ Herbs — Use twice as much fresh herbs as you would with dried herbs to allow for the concentration of flavor resulting from the drying process.

▸ Malts — No difference between homemade and commercial quantities required in recipes.

The use of homemade ingredients can be subtle or loud. When we brew unusual beers such as holiday spice beers or porters, we like to go to town, throwing in as many of our own ingredients as we can get away with. Large, robust beers can take a lot of herbs and spices, but you don't want to use so many that you end up with something that smells or tastes like potpourri. We find that comparatively small amounts of many different ingredients are subtler and more interesting than a big dose of just one or two.

On the other hand, don't overwhelm the beer with too much of a single herb. You need to strike a balance by using just enough, especially in a beer that emphasizes a single herb, for the herbal presence to come through. You want the drinkers to know, for instance, that they are drinking basil beer. But you don't want to dominate your brew with so much of the basil that you feel like all you are drinking is liquid pesto.

As far as homemade malt grains go, they are used exactly the same way as store-bought malts. We tend to stick to a simple grain-and-extract method, although several of the recipes in this chapter call for partial mashing. We include boxes containing all-grain conversions for all our recipes for those interested.

The recipes here have been designed to make the most of your homemade brewing ingredients. Among them are some of our all-time favorite homebrews. Obviously, you can substitute store-bought ingredients in your own brewing; it all depends on what you want to do and what you have time to try. You may want to start out with some of the simpler single-herb recipes such as the dandelion bitter before moving on to more complex ones involving home malting.

Brewing with homegrown ingredients is no more difficult than using any other kind. All the work and worry is involved in the earlier stages of the process; brewing is the reward for your efforts. You may find that growing your own hops, grains, and brewing herbs helps you to produce better and more satisfying beers.

As homebrewers and gardeners, we found growing our own ingredients to be the next logical step in the hobby. Along with all-grain brewing, entering contests, reviving lost styles, and all the other directions being charted by adventurous homebrewers, home growing presents another opportunity for self-expression in homebrewing.

AMAZON BLACK BEER

Amazon black beer is brewed by Brazilian Indians from chewed manioc, a local tuberous root. Our version uses homemade smoked malt to create a dark, velvety, mysterious brew. The taste will carry you away to dark places where the jaguars roam.

YIELD: 5 GALLONS (19 L) • INITIAL GRAVITY: 1.049–1.055 • FINAL GRAVITY: 1.014–1.019

3/4 pound (340 g) 60°L British crystal malt
1/2 pound (227 g) homemade smoked malt
1/4 pound (112 g) roasted barley
1/3 pound (151 g) black patent malt
1 tablespoon (15 ml) gypsum
6.6 pounds (3 kg) Northwest dark malt extract syrup
1 pound (454 g) Munton & Fison light dry malt extract
1/2 pound (227 g) lactose
2 ounces (55 g), Northern Brewer hops AA 9%, HBU 18
Wyeast 1028 London ale or Whitbread ale yeast
2/3 cup (160 ml) corn sugar for priming

1. Crush the malts and add along with the roasted barley and the gypsum to 1½ gallons (6 L) cold water. Bring it to a slow boil over 30 minutes. Strain and rinse with ½ gallon (2 L) 170°F (77°C) water.
2. Add extracts and return to a boil. Add Northern Brewer bittering hops. Boil 40 minutes and add lactose. Boil 20 minutes.
3. Strain hot wort into a fermenter containing 1½ gallons (6 L) of chilled water. Rinse hops with ½ gallon (2 L) pre-boiled water. Top up to 5 gallons (19 L).
4. Pitch yeast when wort cools to 70°F (21°C).
5. Ferment at ale temperatures (65 to 70°F, 18 to 21°C).
6. Fermentation will last 7 to 10 days. Bottle with priming sugar when fermentation ceases. Age 6 to 8 weeks in bottle before drinking.

ALL-GRAIN VERSION

5 pounds (2.3 kg) Klages pale malt
2 pounds (908 g) homemade smoked malt
1 pound (454 g) 60°L British crystal malt
1 pound (454 g) Munich malt
1/2 pound (227 g) black patent malt
1/2 pound (227 g) roasted barley

Mash-in grains at 148°F (64°C) and hold for 90 minutes. Sparge at 170°F (77°C) and collect 5½ gallons (21 L) runoff. Proceed with recipe at start of boil.

DANDELION BITTER

If you have a lawn, dandelions have probably given you a lot of pain over the years. Why not take revenge by using this traditional bittering herb for brewing? This ale is bright brown-orange and cloudy, with a sour piquancy unlike that of hops.

YIELD: 5 GALLONS (19 L) • INITIAL GRAVITY: 1.045–1.056 • FINAL GRAVITY: 1.014–1.018

$\frac{1}{2}$ pound (227 g) toasted malt

$\frac{1}{2}$ pound (227 g) 60°L British crystal malt

3.75 pounds (1.7 kg) Cooper's Bitter kit

2 pounds (908 g) Munton & Fison light dry malt extract

1 pound (454 g) dandelions, leaves, blossoms, and roots

1 ounce (28 g) East Kent Goldings hop plugs for flavoring

$\frac{1}{2}$ ounce (14 g) homegrown Willamette whole hops for flavoring

$\frac{1}{2}$ ounce (14 g) homegrown Willamette whole hops for aroma

Wyeast 1028 London ale or Whitbread ale yeast

$\frac{2}{3}$ cup (160 ml) corn sugar for priming

1. Clean the dandelions very thoroughly in several changes of water, removing any twigs or other debris.

2. Add the malts to 1½ gallons (6 L) cold water and bring to a slow boil over 30 minutes. Strain and rinse with ½ gallon (2 L) 170°F (77°C) water. Add the extracts and return the mixture to a boil. Add dandelions and boil for 45 minutes.

3. Add East Kent Goldings hops for flavoring. Boil for 15 minutes. Add ½ ounce (14 g) Willamette hops for aroma to the last 2 minutes of boil.

4. Strain hot wort into a fermenter containing 1½ gallons (6 L) of chilled water. Rinse hops with ½ gallon (2 L) boiled water. Top up to 5 gallons (19 L).

5. Pitch yeast when wort cools to 70°F (21°C).

6. Ferment at ale temperatures (65 to 70°F, 18 to 21°C). When primary fermentation slows, add ½ ounce (14 g) Willamette dry hops to fermenter.

7. Bottle with priming sugar when fermentation ceases (7 to 10 days). It should be ready to drink in two weeks.

ALL-GRAIN VERSION

5 pounds (2.7 kg) Klages pale malt

1 pound (454 g) toasted malt

$\frac{1}{2}$ pound (227 g) aromatic malt

$\frac{3}{4}$ pound (340 g) home-made crystal malt

Mash-in grains at 153°F (67°C) and hold for 90 minutes. Sparge at 170°F (77°C) and collect 5½ gallons (21 L) runoff. Proceed with recipe.

FRESH HOP ALE

Microbrewer Bert Grant brews a seasonal fresh hop ale. That's right —
undried hops, right off the vine. Homebrewers will have to grow their own for this
experiment. Fresh hops should only be used for aroma or dry hopping, since their
full flavor and bitterness are developed in the drying process. The rule of thumb is to
use six times the amount of fresh hops as dry. Some brewers report grassy flavors
using this method, so brew carefully.

YIELD: 5 GALLONS (19 L) • INITIAL GRAVITY: 1.060–1.065 • FINAL GRAVITY: 1.010–1.015

$^1\!/_2$ pound (227 g) toasted malt

$^3\!/_4$ pound (340 g) 40°L British crystal malt

$^1\!/_4$ pound (112 g) Special B malt

3.3 pounds (1.5 kg) Northwest gold malt extract syrup

$2^1\!/_4$ pounds (1 kg) dry amber spray malt

$^1\!/_2$ ounce (14 g) Chinook hops for bittering, AA 12.7%, HBU 6.35

$^3\!/_4$ ounce (21 g) Cascades hops for flavor

3 ounces (85 g) Willamette fresh hops for aroma

Wyeast 1028 London ale

$^2\!/_3$ cup (160 ml) corn sugar for priming

1. Crush malt and add to $1^1\!/_2$ gallons (6 L) cold water. Bring to a slow boil over 30 minutes. Strain and sparge with $^1\!/_2$ gallon (2 L) 170°F (77°C) water. Add extracts and return to a boil. Add Chinook hops and boil 45 minutes.

2. Add Cascades flavoring hops and boil 5 minutes.

3. Add the fresh Willamette aroma hops and boil for a final 10 minutes.

4. Strain hot wort into a fermenter containing $1^1\!/_2$ gallons of chilled water. Rinse hops with $^1\!/_2$ gallon boiled water. Top up to 5 gallons (19 L).

5. Pitch yeast when cool.

6. Ferment at ale temperatures (65 to 70°F, 18 to 21°C).

7. Bottle with priming sugar when fermentation ceases (7 to 10 days). It should be ready to drink in 2 weeks.

ALL-GRAIN VERSION

$5^1\!/_2$ pounds (2.5 kg) 2-row pale malt

2 pounds (908 g) toasted malt

1 pound (454 g) 40°L British crystal malt

Mash-in grains at 153°F (67°C) and hold for 90 minutes. Sparge at 170°F (77°C) and collect $5^1\!/_2$ gallons (21 L) runoff.

Proceed with recipe at the start of boil.

HONEY BASIL ALE

Yield: 5 gallons (19 L) • Initial Gravity: 1.058–1.062 • Final Gravity: 1.008–1.010

¹/₄ pound (112 g) toasted malt
¹/₃ pound (150 g) wheat malt
³/₄ pound (340 g) 40°L British crystal malt
3 pounds (1.3 kg) Klages pale malt
3 pounds (1.3 kg) honey
1 pound (454 g) Dutch extra light dry malt extract
1 ounce (28 g) Willamette bittering hops, AA 5.3%, HBU 5.3
¹/₂–³/₄ ounce (14–21 g) fresh basil leaves
¹/₂ ounce (14 g) homegrown Willamette leaf hops for aroma
YeastLab A02 American ale yeast
²/₃ cup (160 ml) corn sugar for priming

1. Raise 3½ gallons (13 L) water to 160°F (71°C). Mash-in grains, stabilize at 153°F (67°C) and hold 60 minutes. Sparge at 170°F (77°C) and collect 5½ gallons (21 L) runoff.
2. Add extract and honey to runoff. Bring to a boil and add Willamette bittering hops. Boil 60 minutes. Turn off heat and add basil and aroma hops. Steep 15 minutes.
3. Chill the wort, strain out hops, and transfer to carboy. Pitch yeast when wort cools to 70°F (21°C).
4. Ferment at ale temperatures (65 to 70°F, 18 to 21°C). Bottle with priming sugar when fermentation ceases (1 to 2 weeks).
5. Age 3 weeks before drinking.

ALL-GRAIN VERSION

¹/₂ pound (227 g) toasted malt
¹/₂ pound (227 g) wheat malt
1 pound (454 g) 40°L British crystal malt (454g)
3 pounds (1.3 kg) Klages pale malt
2 pounds (908 g) Munich malt

Raise 3½ gallons (13 L) water to 160°F (71°C). Mash-in grain, stabilize at 153°F (67°C) and hold 60 minutes. Sparge at 170°F (77°C) and collect 5½ gallons (21 L) runoff. Proceed with recipe.

WILD HOPS HONEY ALE

Wild hops are a brewing resource worthy of wider attention. Nameless, feral cultivars escaped from gardens and gone to seed can be a source of subtle aromas and bracing bitterness. We grow a variety of wild Fuggles descended from a bootlegger's private stock. Our brewing friend Brad Hunter found an unknown high-alpha hop growing up the side of an abandoned schoolhouse on Matinicus Island in Maine. Here's what he has to say about this recipe: "A house builder friend of mine was doing a renovation in Rockland, and when one of his crew ripped open the trim on this old house they discovered a huge honey bee nest. He collected all the comb and painstakingly extracted the honey, then didn't know what to do with it, so knowing I brewed, he gave it to me. He got a couple of six-packs in return and it was a really tasty blend of honey, Munich malt toastiness, and a nice hop balance from my Matinicus hops."

YIELD: 5 GALLONS (19 L) • INITIAL GRAVITY: 1.078–1.082 • FINAL GRAVITY: 1.016–1.020

- I pound (454 g) 60°L British crystal malt
- 2 pounds (908 g) Munich malt
- 5¹/₂ pounds (2.5 kg) light dry malt extract
- 4¹/₂ pounds (2 kg) wildflower honey
- 2 ounces (55 g) powdered dextrin
- ¹/₂ teaspoon (14 g) Irish moss
- ¹/₂ ounce (14 g) wild Chinook bittering hops, AA 12.7%, HBU 6.35
- ¹/₂ ounce (14 g) homegrown Cascade whole hops for flavor
- ¹/₂ ounce (14 g) homegrown Cascade whole hops for aroma
  Wyeast 1098 British ale yeast
- ²/₃ cup (160 ml) corn sugar for priming

1. Raise 3½ gallons (13 L) water to 153°F (67°C). Mash-in grain, stabilize at 150°F (67°C) and hold 60 minutes. Sparge at 170°F (77°C) and collect 5½ gallons (21 L) runoff.
2. Add extract and honey to runoff. Boil 40 minutes and add Chinook bittering hops. Boil 20 minutes. Add flavoring hops to final 2 minutes of boil. Turn off heat and add aroma hops. Steep 15 minutes.
3. Chill the wort, strain out hops, and transfer to carboy. Pitch yeast when wort cools to 70°F (21°C).
4. Ferment at ale temperatures (65 to 70°F, 18 to 21°C). Bottle with priming sugar when fermentation ceases (1 to 2 weeks).
5. Age 3 weeks before drinking.

QUINOA BITTER

This brew is a medium-bodied, bracingly bitter, and wonderfully aromatic.

YIELD: 5 GALLONS (19 L) • INITIAL GRAVITY: 1.042–1.048 • FINAL GRAVITY: 1.009–1.012

1/2 pound (227 g) toasted malt

1/3 pound (150 g) biscuit malt

1/4 pound (112 g) aromatic malt

1/2 pound (227 g) raw quinoa

4 pounds (1.8 kg) Alexander's malt extract syrup

1 1/2 pounds (680 g) Dutch extra light dry malt extract

1 ounce (28 g) East Kent Goldings bittering hops AA 4.5%, HBU 4.5

1/2 ounce (14 g) East Kent Goldings flavoring hops

1 ounce (28 g) homegrown Willamette whole hops for flavoring

1/2 ounce (14 g) homegrown Willamette whole hops for aroma

1–2 packets Munton & Fison ale yeast or Wyeast 1028 London ale

2/3 cup (160 ml) corn sugar for priming

1. Rinse the quinoa in cool water to remove its bitterness. Boil it in 1 gallon (4 L) water for 15 minutes, until soft. Add the crushed malts. Stabilize at 150°F (65°C) and hold for 30 minutes. Sparge with 1/2 gallon (2 L) 170°F (77°C) water.

2. Add extracts and return to a boil. Add East Kent Goldings bittering hops and boil 30 minutes. Add flavoring hops and boil 15 minutes. Add Willamette aroma hops to the final 2 minutes of boil.

3. Strain hot wort into a fermenter containing 1 1/2 gallons (6 L) of chilled water. Rinse hops with 1/2 gallon (2 L) boiled water. Top up to 5 gallons (19 L).

4. Pitch yeast when wort cools to 70°F (21°C).

5. Ferment at ale temperatures (65 to 70°F, 18 to 21°C).

6. Bottle when fermentation ceases (7 to 10 days). It should be ready to drink in 2 weeks.

ALL-GRAIN VERSION

1/2 pound (227 g) toasted malt

1/2 pound (227 g) biscuit malt

1/2 pound (227 g) aromatic malt

6 pounds (2.7 kg) quinoa

5 pounds (2.3 kg) 6-row pale malt

Boil quinoa 30 minutes with 3 1/2 gallons (13 L) water. Mash-in grain, stabilize at 122°F (50°C) and hold for 30 minutes. Raise the temperature to 153°F (67°C) and hold until conversion is complete, 45 minutes. Sparge at 170°F (77°C) and collect 6 gallons (23 L) runoff.

HOREHOUND BROWN ALE

Horehound ale is a traditional English drink. Frances Bardswell wrote in 1911,
"Horehound is bitter with quite a different bitterness. In Norfolk many a cottage has its
Horehound corner, and Horehound beer is brewed and drunk." When experimenting with
horehound, it is best to start with small amounts. This is a very bitter herb.

YIELD: 5 GALLONS (19 L) • INITIAL GRAVITY: 1.042–1.055 • FINAL GRAVITY: 1.015–1.019

½ pound (227 g) 60°L British crystal malt (220 g)

4 pounds (1.8 kg) Mahogany Coast Nut Brown ale kit

2 pounds (908 g) Munton & Fison dark dry malt extract

½ cup (120 ml) molasses

2 ounces (57 g) fresh horehound leaves or 1 ounce (28 g) dry

1 ounce (28 g) fresh ginger root, grated

½ ounce (14 g) East Kent Goldings hop plug for flavoring

1 packet Whitbread ale yeast or Wyeast 1028 London ale

⅔ cup (160 ml) corn sugar for priming

1. Add the crushed malt to 1½ gallons (6 L) cold water. Bring to a slow boil over 30 minutes. Strain and rinse with ½ gallon (2 L) boiled water 170°F (77°C) water. Add extracts and molasses and return to a boil. Add the horehound and ginger and boil 45 minutes.

2. Add East Kent Goldings flavoring hops and boil 15 minutes.

3. Strain hot wort into a fermenter containing 1½ gallons (6 L) of chilled water. Rinse hops with ½ gallon (2 L) boiled water. Top up to 5 gallons (19 L).

4. Pitch yeast when wort cools to 70°F (21°C).

5. Ferment at ale temperatures (65 to 70°F, 18 to 21°C). When primary fermentation slows, add ½ ounce (14 g) Willamette dry hops to the fermenter.

6. Bottle with priming sugar when fermentation ceases (7 to 10 days). It should be ready to drink in 2 weeks.

ALL-GRAIN VERSION

½ pound (227 g) chocolate malt

1 pound (454 g) 60°L British crystal malt

2 pounds (908 g) Munich malt

3½ pounds (1.6 kg) biscuit malt or Klages malt

Mash-in grains at 153°F (67°C) and hold for 90 minutes. Sparge at 170°F (77°C) and collect 5½ gallons (21 L) runoff. Proceed with recipe.

CHICHA DE JORA

Chicha is the corn ale of the Andes, brewed by the Quechua Indians of Peru at least since the time of the Inca empire. It's still being brewed there today, using the same methods. Traditionally, it's consumed warm, at the frothy height of its fermentation, but the brew is supposed to gain strength when stored underground. Fresh chicha is opaque yellow, tart, and as refreshing as cider or Belgian lambic. If allowed to age in the bottle, chicha eventually turns into something that looks and tastes like undistilled sour mash whiskey. Sometimes fresh strawberries are added to fermenting chicha to make a drink called frutillada. Two or three pounds (.9 to 1.4 kg) of berries added to the primary fermentation is a good place to start experimenting at copying this age-old treat.

YIELD: 1 GALLON (4 L) • INITIAL GRAVITY: 1.048–1.060 • FINAL GRAVITY: 1.010–1.013

> 4 pounds (1.8 kg) malted corn
> 1/4 pound (112 g) brown sugar
> 16 ounces (460 ml) homebrewed porter
> 2 bags Celestial Seasonings Tension Tamer tea
> 1 packet Munton & Fison ale yeast
> 1/4 cup (60 ml) corn sugar for priming

1. Crush the malt. Add 1 gallon (4 L) boiling water. Stir the mash well and let it sit for 1 hour. Drain off the sweet liquor and add more boiling water to the mash. Drain off the sweet liquor. There should be a total of 1½ to 1¾ gallons (6 to 7 L) of runoff.

2. Bring the runoff to a boil and add the sugar and beer. Boil for approximately 3 hours, until only 1 gallon (4 L) of wort is left. Add the tea bags to the cooling wort.

3. Pour the wort into a fermenter (a sanitized milk jug makes a nice 1 gallon (4 L) fermenter; a size 6½ stopper fits the neck exactly).

4. Pitch the yeast when wort cools to 70°F (21°C).

5. Ferment at 60 to 70°F (15 to 21°C). Although usually consumed before it has finished fermenting, chicha can be bottled with priming sugar and aged.

CHILI BEER

YIELD: 5 GALLONS (19 L) • INITIAL GRAVITY: 1.049–1.055 • FINAL GRAVITY: 1.010–1.016

¹/₂ pound (227 g) toasted pale malt

¹/₈ pound (55 g) homemade smoked malt

5 pounds (2.3 kg) Dutch extra light dry malt extract

¹/₂ pound (227 g) honey

1 ounce (28 g) Hallertauer hop pellets for bittering, AA 5%, HBU 5

1–4 dried hot chili peppers

2–6 fresh ripe Thai hot chili peppers

¹/₄ pound (112 g) fresh or frozen roasted Jalapeño peppers

1 packet European lager yeast or YeastLab L31 Pilsner lager yeast

³/₄ cup (180 ml) corn sugar for priming

1. Toast the pale malt in a 350°F (178°C) oven for 5 to 10 minutes, until golden and aromatic. Allow it to cool and crush it.
2. Add the malt to 1½ gallons (6 L) cold water and bring to a slow boil over 30 minutes. Strain and rinse with ½ gallon (2 L) 170°F (77°C) water. Add the extract and honey and return the mixture to a boil.
3. Add 1 ounce (28 g) Hallertauer hops for bittering and 1–4 dried hot chili peppers. Boil 40 minutes. Add 2–6 fresh ripe Thai hot chili peppers. Boil 20 minutes.
4. Turn off the heat and add ¼ pound (114 g) frozen roasted Jalapeño peppers. Allow the wort to steep for 15 to 20 minutes, then pour the entire mixture into a 6½ gallon (25 L) plastic fermenting bucket with 1½ gallons (6 L) chilled water.
5. Top up to 5½ gallons (21 L) and pitch yeast when wort cools to at least 50°F (10°C).
6. Allow the beer and peppers to ferment together for at least 2 weeks to a month at lager temperatures (40 to 50°F, 4 to 10°C). Then strain out the peppers and rack the beer to a carboy to complete fermentation.
7. Bottle when secondary fermentation is complete. Age 6 to 8 weeks in the bottle before drinking.

ALL-GRAIN VERSION

6 pounds (2.7 kg) pale malt

¹/₂ pound (227 g) homemade smoked malt

³/₄ pound (340 g) toasted malt

Mash-in grains, stabilize at 122°F (50°C) and hold for 30 minutes. Raise the temperature to 153°F (67°C) and hold until conversion is complete, 45 minutes. Sparge at 170°F (77°C) and collect 5½ gallons (21 L) runoff. Proceed with recipe at hop additions.

AMARANTH EXTRA SPECIAL BITTER

Amaranth Extra Special Bitter combines a high, hoppy nose, clear amber color, and foamy head with assertive hoppiness.

YIELD: 5 GALLONS (19 L) • INITIAL GRAVITY: 1.049–1.055 • FINAL GRAVITY: 1.014–1.018

> 6 ounces (168 g) malted amaranth
>
> 3.3 pounds (1.5 kg) Northwest gold malt extract syrup
>
> 2.2 pounds (1 kg) Premier pale hopped malt extract
>
> 1 pound (454 g) Munton & Fison pale dried malt extract
>
> 1 ounce (28 g) Cascade hops for bittering, AA 6%, HBU 12
>
> 3/4 ounce (21 g) East Kent Goldings hops for bittering, AA 4.5%, HBU 3.375
>
> 1/2 ounce (14 g) Cascade homegrown whole hops for flavoring
>
> 3/4 ounce (21 g) East Kent Goldings hops for flavoring
>
> 1/2 ounce (14 g) homegrown Cascade leaf hops for aroma
>
> 1/2 ounce (14 g) homegrown Willamette dry hops
>
> 1 packet Wyeast 1028 London ale or 1 packet Edme ale yeast
>
> 2/3 cup (160 ml) corn sugar for priming

1. Crush the amaranth malt in a zip-seal bag. Add the malt to 1½ gallons (6 L) cold water and bring to a boil over 30 minutes. Strain and rinse with ½ gallon (2 L) 170°F (77°C) water. Add the extracts and return the mixture to a boil. Add 1 ounce (28 g) Cascade hops and ¾ ounce (21 g) East Kent Goldings hops. Boil for 30 minutes.

2. Add ½ ounce (14 g) Cascade hops and ¾ ounce (21 g) East Kent Goldings hops. Boil for 15 minutes. Add ½ ounce (14 g) Cascade hops the last 2 minutes of boil.

3. Strain hot wort into a fermenter containing 1½ gallons (6 L) of chilled water. Rinse hops with ½ gallon (2 L) boiled water. Top up to 5 gallons (19 L).

4. Pitch yeast when wort cools to 70°F (21°C).

5. Ferment at ale temperatures (65 to 70°F, 18 to 21°C). When primary fermentation slows, add ½ ounces (14 g) Willamette dry hops to fermenter.

6. Bottle with priming sugar when fermentation ceases (7 to 10 days). It should be ready to drink in 2 weeks, but will smooth out with age.

ALL-GRAIN VERSION

> 5 pounds (2.3 kg) Klages malt
>
> 6 pounds (2.7 kg) malted amaranth

Mash-in grain, stabilize at 122°F (50°C), and hold for 30 minutes. Raise the temperature to 153°F (67°C) and hold until conversion is complete, 45 minutes. Sparge at 170°F (77°C)

MIXED BERRY PORTER

YIELD: 5 GALLONS (19 L) • INITIAL GRAVITY: 1.060–1.072 • FINAL GRAVITY: 1.016–1.020

1/2 pound (227 g) 60°L British crystal malt

1/2 pound (227 g) chocolate malt

1/3 pound (150 g) roasted malt

1/3 pound (150 g) black patent malt

1/4 pound (112 g) homemade smoked malt

3.75 pounds (1.7 kg) Black Rock Miner's Stout kit

3.3 pounds (1.5 kg) Northwest amber malt extract syrup

1 ounce (28 g) East Kent Goldings hop plugs, AA 4.5%, HBU 4.5

1 licorice root

6 pounds (2.7 kg) mixed blackberries, raspberries, and elderberries, crushed

1 packet Whitbread ale yeast or YeastLab A05 Irish Ale yeast

1/2 cup (120 ml) corn sugar for priming

1. Add the crushed malts to 1½ gallons (6 L) cold water and bring to a slow boil over 30 minutes. Strain and rinse with ½ gallon (2 L) 170°F (77°C) water. Add the extracts and return the mixture to a boil.

2. Add the East Kent Goldings hop plugs and licorice. Boil 60 minutes.

3. Turn off the heat and add fruit. Allow the wort to steep for 15 to 20 minutes, then pour the entire mixture into a 6½ gallon (25 L) plastic fermenting bucket with 1½ gallons (6 L) chilled water.

4. Top up to 5½ gallons (21 L) and pitch yeast when wort cools to at least 70°F (21°C).

5. Allow the beer and fruit to ferment together for at least two weeks to a month at ale temperatures (65 to 70°F, 18 to 21°C). Then rack the beer to a carboy to complete its fermentation.

6. Bottle with priming sugar when fermentation is complete. Age 3 weeks before drinking.

ALL-GRAIN VERSION

2 pounds (908 g) Munich malt

1 pound (454 g) toasted malt

6 pounds (2.7 kg) Klages pale malt

1 pound (454 g) homemade crystal malt

1/2 pound (227 g) smoked malt

1/2 pound (227 g) roasted barley

1/2 pound (227 g) black patent malt

Mash-in grains at 148°F (64°C) and hold for 90 minutes. Sparge at 170°F (77°C) and collect 5½ gallons (21 L) runoff. Proceed with recipe.

RHUBARB ALE

Yield: 5 gallons (19 L) • Initial Gravity: 1.053–1.062 • Final Gravity: 1.014–1.020

- ¹/₈ pound (55 g) roasted barley
- ¹/₂ pound (227 g) homemade crystal malt
- ¹/₃ pound (150 g) Special B malt
- ¹/₃ pound (150 g) steel-cut oats
- ¹/₄ pound (112 g) rye malt
- 4 pounds (1.8 kg) Dogbolter Bitter kit
- 3.3 pounds (1.5 kg) Northwest gold malt extract syrup
- ¹/₂ ounce (14 g) East Kent Goldings hop plug, AA 4.5%, HBU 2.25
- 1 ounce (28 g) rosemary or hyssop
- 1 ounce (28 g) betony or clary sage
- 1 ounce (28 g) bee balm
- 6 pounds (2.7 kg) rhubarb stalks, chopped
- 1 packet Wyeast 1028 London ale or Whitbread ale yeast
- ¹/₂ cup (120 ml) corn sugar for priming

1. Add crushed malts to 1½ gallons (6 L) cold water. Bring to a boil over 30 minutes. Strain and rinse with ½ gallon (2 L) 170°F (77°C) water.
2. Add extracts and bring to a boil. Add ½ ounce (14 g) East Kent Goldings bittering hops, rosemary or hyssop, and betony or clary sage. Boil 60 minutes. Add bee balm to the last 5 minutes of boil.
3. Turn off the heat and add rhubarb. Allow the wort to steep for 15 to 20 minutes, then pour whole mixture into a 6½ gallon (25 L) plastic fermenting bucket containing 1½ gallons (6 L) chilled water.
4. Top up to 5½ gallons (21 L) and pitch yeast when wort cools to 70°F (21°C).
5. Allow the beer and fruit to ferment together for at least 2 weeks to a month at ale temperatures (65 to 70°F, 18 to 21°C). Then rack the beer to a carboy to complete its fermentation.
6. Bottle with priming sugar when fermentation is complete. Age three weeks in the bottle before drinking.

ALL-GRAIN VERSION

- 7 pounds (3 kg) Klages malt
- 1¹/₂ pounds (680 g) homemade crystal malt
- 2 pounds (908 g) rye malt
- 2 pounds (908 g) steel-cut oats
- ¹/₂ pound (227 g) roasted barley

Mash-in the grains with 3⅕ gallons 148°F (64°C) water and hold for 2 hours. Sparge at 170°F (77°C) and collect 5½ gallons (21 L) runoff. Proceed with recipe.

WINTER WASSAIL

This Christmas ale combines cranberries with spices and honey for a warming delight.

YIELD: 5 GALLONS (19 L) • INITIAL GRAVITY: 1.059–1.066 • FINAL GRAVITY: 1.010–1.014

- ⅛ pound (55 g) roasted malt
- ½ pound (227 g) crystal malt
- 3.3 pounds (1.5 kg) Northwest gold extract syrup
- 2 pounds (908 g) Munton & Fison pale dry malt extract
- 2 pounds (908 g) honey
- 1 ounce (28 g) Cascade hops for bittering, AA 6%, HBU 12
- ½ ounce (14 g) ground coriander seed
- ½ ounce (14 g) homegrown Cascade leaf hops for flavoring
- ½ ounce (14 g) Saaz hop plug
- 6 inch (15 cm) stick cinnamon
- zest from 4 oranges
- 4 pounds (1.8 kg) crushed fresh or frozen cranberries
- 2 pounds (908 g) ground tart apples or crabapples
- 1 packet Wyeast 1028 London ale
- ⅔ cup (160 ml) corn sugar for priming

1. Add crushed malts to 1½ gallons (6 L) cold water. Bring to a boil over 30 minutes. Strain and rinse with ½ gallon (2 L) 170°F (77°C) water.

2. Add extracts and honey and bring to a boil. Boil 20 minutes and add 1 ounce (28 g) Cascade hops. Boil 20 more minutes; then add ¼ ounce (7 g) coriander seed and ½ ounce (14 g) homegrown Cascade hops. Boil 10 minutes; then add remaining coriander, cinnamon, and orange zest. Add Saaz hops to the final 2 minutes of boil.

3. Turn off the heat and add crushed fruit. Allow the wort to steep for 15 to 20 minutes, then pour into a 6½ gallon (25 L) plastic fermenting bucket with 1½ gallons (6 L) chilled water.

4. Top up to 5½ gallons (21 L) and pitch yeast when wort cools to 70°F (21°C).

5. Allow the beer and fruit to ferment together for at least 2 weeks to a month at ale temperatures (65 to 70°F, 18 to 21°C). Rack the beer to a carboy to complete its fermentation.

6. Bottle when fermentation is complete. Age 3 weeks before drinking.

ALL-GRAIN VERSION

- 7 pounds (3 kg) Klages malt
- ¾ pound (340 g) 60°L British crystal malt
- ¼ pound (112 g) roasted barley

Mash-in grains, stabilize at 122°F (50°C) and hold for 30 minutes. Raise the temperature to 153°F (67°C) and hold 30 minutes. Sparge at 170°F (77°C) and collect 5½ gallons (21 L) runoff. Proceed with recipe.

GINGERED ALE

YIELD: 5 GALLONS (19 L) • INITIAL GRAVITY: 1.048–1.052 • FINAL GRAVITY: 1.010–1.012

3/4 pound (340 g) homemade crystal malt

1/3 pound (150 g) homemade roasted barley

1/4 pound (112 g) rye malt

4 pounds (1.8 kg) Mahogany Coast Nut Brown Ale kit

1 1/2 pounds (680 g) Munton & Fison light dry malt extract

1 cup (230 ml) sorghum syrup or molasses

1 1/2 ounces (42 g) Cascade bittering hops, AA 6%, HBU 9

6 inch (15 cm) licorice root

2–4 ounces (55–112 g) fresh grated ginger

1–3 stars of star anise

1/2 ounce (14 g) homegrown Willamette hops for aroma

1 packet Wyeast 1028 London ale or Whitbread or Munton & Fison ale yeast

2/3 cup (160 ml) corn sugar for priming

1. Add crushed malts to 1½ gallons (6 L) cold water. Bring to a boil over 30 minutes. Strain and rinse with ½ gallon (2 L) 170°F (77°C) water.

2. Add extracts and sorghum syrup and bring to a boil. Add 1½ ounces (42 g) Cascade bittering hops, licorice root, ginger, and star anise and boil 60 minutes. Add ½ ounce (14 g) Willamette hops to final 2 minutes of boil.

3. Strain hot wort into a fermenter containing 1½ gallons (6 L) of chilled water. Rinse with ½ gallon (2 L) boiled water. Top up to 5 gallons (19 L).

4. Pitch yeast when wort cools to 70°F (21°C).

5. Ferment at ale temperatures (65 to 70°F, 18 to 21°C). Bottle with priming sugar when fermentation ceases (1 to 2 weeks).

6. Age 3 weeks before drinking.

ALL-GRAIN VERSION

1 pound (454 g) homemade crystal malt

3/4 pound (340 g) rye malt

6 pounds (2.7 kg) Klages pale malt

1 pound (454 g) toasted malt

1/2 pound (227 g) roasted barley

Mash-in grains, stabilize at 122°F (50°C), and hold for 30 minutes. Raise the temperature to 153°F (67°C) and hold 30 minutes. Sparge at 170°F (77°C) and collect 5½ gallons (21 L) runoff. Proceed with recipe.

GOTLANDSDRIKA

Gotlandsdrika is an ancient beverage, the original homebrew of Scandinavia. It's made with smoked barley malt, juniper branches, rye, wheat, and other fermentables. It comes from the island of Gotland in the Baltic Sea, hence its name.

YIELD: 5 GALLONS (19 L) • INITIAL GRAVITY: 1.055–1.062 • FINAL GRAVITY: 1.009–1.012

> 2 pounds (908 g) homemade smoked malt
> ½ pound (227 g) homemade crystal malt
> ⅓ pound (150 g) rye malt
> ⅓ pound (150 g) wheat malt
> 6–8 inch (15–20 cm) juniper branch
> 3.3 pounds (1.5 kg) BierKeller light malt extract syrup
> 2 pounds (908 g) Munton & Fison dry wheat malt extract
> 1 pound (454 g) honey
> ⅓ ounce (9 g) Perle hops, AA 8%, HBU 2.4
> 1 packet Nottingham ale yeast or Wyeast 1028 London ale
> ½ cup (120 ml) corn sugar for priming

1. Pour 1 gallon (4 L) boiling water over the crushed malts and juniper branch. Allow to sit overnight covered, then strain and rinse with ½ gallon (2 L) 170°F (77°C) water.
2. Add extracts and honey and bring to a boil. Add ⅓ ounce (9 g) Perle hops and boil 1 hour.
3. Strain hot wort into a fermenter containing 1½ gallons (6 L) of chilled water. Rinse with ½ gallon (2 L) boiled water. Top up to 5 gallons (19 L).
4. Pitch yeast when wort cools to 70°F (21°C).
5. Ferment at ale temperatures (65 to 70°F, 18 to 21°C). Bottle with priming sugar when fermentation ceases (1 to 2 weeks).
6. Age 3 weeks before drinking.

ALL-GRAIN VERSION

5 pounds (2.3 kg) homemade smoked barley

Boil 8 gallons water with juniper branch for 1 hour. Mash-in grains and hold for 90 minutes at 154°F (68°C). Sparge with juniper water at 190°F (88°C). Collect 5 gallons (19 L) runoff. Add honey and proceed with hop additions.

HEATHER ALE

According to legend, the last remaining member of the pre-Celtic tribe of Picts jumped to his death rather than hand over the recipe for heather ale to a Scottish king, and so the secret of making ale from heather blossoms was lost forever. In fact, heather ale is being brewed commercially again in Scotland and is experiencing a revival. In order to get enough heather for this recipe, you'll need at least one dozen plants, or a local source of dried blossoms.

YIELD: 5 GALLONS (19 L) • INITIAL GRAVITY: 1.048–1.060 • FINAL GRAVITY: 1.011–1.015

$^1/_4$ **pound (112 g) toasted malt**
$^1/_3$ **pound (150 g) biscuit malt**
$^1/_2$ **pound (227 g) homemade crystal malt**
$^1/_4$ **pound (112 g) Special B malt**
 4 pounds (1.8 kg) Geordie Scottish Export kit
 2 pounds (908 g) Munton & Fison light dry malt extract
 12 cups (2.8 L) dried heather blossoms
 1 sprig dried heather for "dry hopping"
 Wyeast #1728 Scottish Ale yeast
$^2/_3$ **cup (160 ml) corn sugar for priming**

1. Add the crushed malts to 1½ gallons (6 L) cold water and bring to a slow boil over 30 minutes. Strain and rinse with ½ gallon (2 L) 170°F (77°C) water. Add the extracts and return the mixture to a boil.

2. Add 10 cups heather blossoms. Boil 90 minutes. Put the remaining 2 cups heather blossoms in a strainer. Strain the hot wort through it into a fermenter containing 1½ gallons (6 L) of chilled water. Rinse with ½ gallon (2 L) boiled water. Top up to 5 gallons (19 L).

3. Pitch yeast when wort cools to 70°F (21°C).

4. Ferment at ale temperatures (65 to 70°F, 18 to 21°C). When fermentation slows, add 1 sprig dried heather. Bottle with priming sugar when fermentation ceases (2 to 6 weeks).

5. Age 3 to 6 weeks before drinking.

ALL-GRAIN VERSION

 6 **pounds (2.7 kg) Scotch ale malt or 2-row pale malt**
$^1/_2$ **pound (227 g) biscuit malt**
$^3/_4$ **pound (340 g) homemade crystal malt**
$^1/_2$ **pound (227 g) toasted malt**
$^1/_4$ **pound (112 g) Special B malt**

Mash-in grains at 153°F (67°C) and hold for 90 minutes. Sparge at 170°F (77°C) and collect 5½ gallons (21 L) runoff. Proceed with recipe.

MUMM

Mumm is an original ale, from the days when ale meant a black brew bittered with the local herbs and no hops. It was being brewed in Britain and Brunswick, Germany, in 1600 and was a favorite of the Hanoverian kings of England. A highly individualistic style, Mumm can be flavored with any of the herbs in the recipe, or whatever others suggest themselves. There's no describing the flavor of Mumm; malty, spicy, warming, and bitter, it suggests an alcoholic version of Moxie or Dr. Pepper, without the cloying sweetness. Mumm will need to sit a while in your cellar to mellow — it is a beer that will definitely benefit from aging.

YIELD: 5 GALLONS (19 L) • INITIAL GRAVITY: 1.055–1.062 • FINAL GRAVITY: 1.014–1.018

- ³/₄ pound (340 g) 60°L British crystal malt
- ¹/₃ pound (150 g) wheat malt
- 1¹/₂ pounds (680 g) steel-cut oats
- ¹/₄ pound (112 g) rye malt
- ¹/₄ pound (112 g) black patent malt
- ¹/₄ pound (112 g) homemade roasted malt
- 3.3 pounds (1.5 kg) Northwest gold malt extract syrup
- 3.3 pounds (1.5 kg) Northwest wheat malt extract syrup
- 1 ounce (28 g) Northern Brewer hops, AA 9%, HBU 9
- 1 packet Wyeast 3068 Weihenstephan wheat yeast or Whitbread ale yeast
- ²/₃ cup (160 ml) corn sugar for priming

Any 6 of the following:

- 2 tablespoons (30 ml) fresh juniper berries
- ¹/₄ cup (60 ml) sunflower seeds
- ¹/₂ ounce (14 g) fresh blue spruce tips
- ¹/₄ ounce (7 g) fresh birch tips
- ¹/₂ ounce (14 g) dried nettles
- 1 ounce (28 g) fresh betony
- 1 ounce (28 g) fresh marjoram
- 6 bay leaves
- 1 ounce (28 g) fresh alecost
- 1 ounce (28 g) fresh rosemary
- 1 ounce (28 g) fresh hyssop
- ¹/₂ ounce (14 g) dried chamomile
- ¹/₂ ounce (14 g) dried rose hips
- ¹/₄ ounce (7 g) fresh lavender flowers
- ¹/₄ ounce (7 g) fresh elder flowers

¼ ounce (7 g) elecampane root
1 licorice root (dried)
1 tablespoon (15 ml) fennel seed

1. Add the crushed malts to 1½ gallons (6 L) cold water and bring to a slow boil over 30 minutes. Strain and rinse with ½ (2 L) gallon 170°F (77°C) boiled water. Add the extracts and return the mixture to a boil.

2. Add 1 ounce (28 g) Northern Brewer hops and spices of your choice. Boil 60 minutes.

3. Strain the hot wort into a fermenter containing 1½ gallons (6 L) of chilled water. Rinse with ½ gallon (2 L) boiled water. Top up to 5 gallons (19 L).

4. Pitch yeast when wort cools to 70°F (21°C).

5. Ferment at ale temperatures (65 to 70°F, 18 to 21°C). Bottle with priming sugar when fermentation ceases (1 to 2 weeks).

6. Age at least 3 to 6 weeks before drinking.

ALL-GRAIN VERSION

5 pounds (2.3 kg) Klages malt
1½ pounds (680 g) home-made crystal malt
3 pounds (1.3 kg) rye malt
2 pounds (908 g) wheat malt
2 pounds (908 g) steel-cut oats
½ pound (227 g) roasted barley
⅓ pound (150 g) black patent malt

Mash-in the grains with 3½ gallons (13 L) 148°F (64°C) water and hold for 2 hours. Sparge at 170°F (77°C) and collect 5½ gallons (21 L) runoff. Proceed with recipe.

AGE TO SAVE

Patience is a real virtue when dealing with a beer that has been slightly over-herbed. We know someone who made a spruce porter that tasted at first like turpentine. After a few years of aging (it was a strong porter), the flavor mellowed and improved. Our first attempt at a chili beer had similar results — it took months for the fiery tang to abate enough for our tastes. Remember that historical herbal beers like Mumm were supposed to age for years. So if your beer brewed with homemade ingredients seems undrinkable at first, don't panic. It may mature into a very acceptable — even a superior — product.

OREGANO PALE ALE

This beer is our interpretation of Pike Place Brewery's Birra Perfetto. This hoppy traditional pale ale spiced with oregano is malty, earthy, and smoother than you'd think possible.

YIELD: 5 GALLONS (19 L) • INITIAL GRAVITY: 1.048–1.057 • FINAL GRAVITY: 1.012–1.016

- ¼ pound (112 g) toasted malt
- ¼ pound (112 g) Cara-Pils malt
- ½ pound (227 g) 60°L British crystal malt
- ½ pound (227 g) 40°L British crystal malt
- 6.6 pounds (3 kg) Northwest gold malt extract syrup
- 1¼ pounds (560 g) Dutch extra light dry malt extract
- 2 ounces (55 g) East Kent Goldings hops for bittering, AA 4.5%, HBU 9
- 1 ounce (28 g) Fuggles hops for bittering, AA 4%, HBU 4
- 1 ounce (28 g) fresh oregano
- ½ ounce (14 g) homegrown Fuggles whole hops for flavoring
- ½ ounce (14 g) homegrown Willamette whole hops for aroma
  YeastLab A02 American Ale
- 1 sprig fresh oregano
- ⅔ cup (160 ml) corn sugar for priming

1. Add the crushed malts to 1½ gallons (6 L) cold water and bring to a slow boil over 30 minutes. Strain and rinse with ½ gallon (2 L) 170°F (77°C) boiled water. Add the extracts and return the mixture to a boil.
2. Add 2 ounces (57 g) East Kent Goldings and 1 ounce (28 g) Fuggles bittering hops. Boil 45 minutes. Add oregano and ½ ounce (14 g) Fuggles hops and boil 15 minutes. Add ½ ounce (14 g) aroma hops to final 2 minutes of boil.
3. Strain the hot wort into a fermenter containing 1½ gallons (6 L) chilled water. Rinse the hops with ½ gallon (2 L) boiled water. Top up to 5 gallons. Pitch the yeast when wort cools to 70°F (21°C).
4. Ferment at ale temperatures (65 to 70°F, 18 to 21°C). When fermentation slows (1 to 3 days), add oregano. Bottle when fermentation is done.
5. Age 4 to 6 weeks before drinking.

ALL-GRAIN VERSION

- 6 pounds (2.7 kg) Klages pale malt
- 1 pound (454 g) toasted malt
- ¾ pound (340 g) Munich malt
- ½ pound (227 g) aromatic malt
- ¾ pound (350 g) 60°L British crystal malt
- ½ pound (227 g) 40°L British crystal malt

Mash-in grains at 153°F (67°C) and hold for 90 minutes. Sparge at 170°F (77°C) and collect 5½ gallons (21 L) runoff. Proceed with recipe.

PUMPKIN ALE

Pumpkin Ale was a favorite of Thomas Jefferson and has enjoyed a revival lately thanks to microbrewers like "Buffalo" Bill Owens. Our version is clear copper-orange with a creamy head, spicy nose, pumpkin sweetness, and gingery, warming bite.

YIELD: 5 GALLONS (19 L) • INITIAL GRAVITY: 1.069–1.072 • FINAL GRAVITY: 1.012–1.018

2 pounds (908 g) pale 6-row malt

1 pound (454 g) homemade crystal malt

1/2 pound (227 g) toasted malt

8 pounds (3.6 kg) fresh pumpkin

6.6 pounds (2.7 kg) Northwest gold malt extract syrup

1/2 p'1ound (227 g) honey

1 teaspoon (14 g) Irish moss

1 ounce (28 g) Northern Brewer hops for bittering,
AA 9%, HBU 9

1/4 ounce (7 g) fresh ginger, grated

1 stick cinnamon

5 whole allspice berries

4 whole cloves

1 teaspoon (5 ml) nutmeg

1 ounce (28 g) homegrown Fuggles hops for aroma

1/2 ounce (14 g) homegrown Willamette dry hops

1–2 packets Edme ale yeast or YeastLab A02 American Ale

3/4 cup (180 ml) corn sugar for priming

1. Clean and section a 10-pound (4.5 kg) pumpkin. Small pie-pumpkin varieties such as Young's Beauty or New England Pie work much better than larger jack-o-lantern types, because the flesh is denser with a higher level of sugar. (In a pinch, winter squash such as acorn squash can be substituted.) After the seeds, pulp, and rind are removed, you should have 8 pounds (3.6 kg) of usable flesh. Bake the pumpkin at 350°F (178°C) for 1¼ hours. This will gelatinize the starches, allowing them to be broken down by malt enzymes into fermentable sugars and dextrins. Grind and mash the baked pumpkin into pulp.

2. Crush the grains. Soak them in 1 gallon (4 L) of cold water for 5 minutes. Add the pumpkin. Slowly raise the mash temperature to 150°F (65°C) and hold for 30 minutes. Sparge with ½ gallon (2 L) 170°F (77°C) water.

3. Add extracts, honey, Irish moss, and 1 ounce (28 g) Northern Brewer bittering hops. Boil 30 minutes. Add spices and boil 15 minutes. Add ½ ounce (14 g) Fuggles finishing hops to the final 2 minutes of boil.

4. Strain hot wort into a fermenter containing 1½ gallons (6 L) chilled water. Rinse the hops with ½ gallon (2 L) boiled water. Top up to 5 gallons (19 L). Pitch the yeast when wort cools to 70°F (21°C).

5. Ferment at ale temperatures (65 to 70°F, 18 to 21°C). After primary fermentation stops (1 to 3 days), add ½ ounce (14 g) Willamette dry hops. Bottle with priming sugar when fermentation is complete.

6. Age 4 to 6 weeks before drinking.

ALL-GRAIN VERSION

10 **pounds (4.5 kg) 2-row pale malt**

1 **pound (454 g) homemade crystal malt**

½ **pound (227 g) toasted malt**

Mash grains at 152°F (67°C). Add baked pumpkin (see below) and stabilize temperature at 152°F (67°C). Hold for 1 hour. Sparge at 170°F (77°C) and collect 5½ gallons (21 L) runoff. Proceed with recipe.

THE RENEWABLE BREWER: HOW TO GET RID OF BREWING BY-PRODUCTS IN EARTH-FRIENDLY WAYS

▸ Baking — A portion of your spent grains can be baked into homemade bread and cookies. Make sure to completely dry out the grains in an oven before reusing them as an ingredient.

▸ Composting — Spent grains and yeast make great additions to your compost pile.

▸ Animal Feed — If you live in a rural area, you can easily find a pig farmer who will be happy to take spent grains off your hands. Pigs also love spent yeast or any spoiled batches of beer. We learned this by sad experience when a group of semi-feral pigs got into our compost bin, tore it into tangled wire, and then proceeded to root up the lawn.

▸ Slug Bait — Spent yeast is better than beer for making organic slug baits. Pour a cupful or two into old margarine tubs and space them around the garden at about 10-foot (3 m) intervals. Slugs will happily drown themselves in them. Refill every month or so throughout the season.

▸ Mulch — You might also consider using spent grains as mulch in your garden or around the bases of shrubs and trees. People use cocoa hulls for this purpose, which are not dissimilar from barley grains. The problem is that, like cocoa hulls, they tend to dry up and blow away.

ROGGENBIER

Roggen, or "rye" beer, is a German ale that predates the Reinheitsgebot, *according to its producer, Bavaria's Shierlinger brewery. The* Reinheitsgebot *is the German law enacted in 1516 forbidding the use of any ingredients but malt, hops, and yeast in beer.*

YIELD: 5 GALLONS (19 L) • INITIAL GRAVITY: 1.062–1.068 • FINAL GRAVITY: 1.012–1.019

½ pound (227 g) Munich malt
½ pound (227 g) 90°L German crystal malt
⅓ pound (150 g) homemade crystal malt
⅓ pound (150 g) Cara-Pils malt
⅓ pound (150 g) aromatic malt
½ pound (227 g) rye malt
½ pound (227 g) flaked rye
4 pounds (1.8 kg) Laaglander Dutch Light Lager kit
2 pounds (908 kg) Dutch extra light dry malt extract
1 ounce (28 g) Perle bittering hops, AA 8%, HBU 8
½ ounce (14 g) homegrown Perle flavoring hops
Wyeast #3056 Bavarian weissen yeast
¾ cup (180 ml) corn sugar for priming

1. Add the crushed malts to 1½ gallons (6 L) cold water and bring to a slow boil over 30 minutes. Strain and rinse with ½ gallon (2 L) 170°F (77°C) water. Add the extracts and return the mixture to a boil.
2. Add 1 ounce (28 g) Perle bittering hops and boil 60 minutes. Add ½ ounce (14 g) Perle flavoring hops to final 10 minutes of boil.
3. Strain hot wort into a fermenter containing 1½ gallons (6 L) of chilled water. Rinse with ½ gallon (2 L) boiled water. Top up to 5 gallons (19 L).
4. Pitch yeast when wort cools to 70°F (21°C).
5. Ferment at ale temperatures (65 to 70°F, 18 to 21°C). Bottle with priming sugar when fermentation ceases (1 to 2 weeks).
6. Age 3 to 6 weeks before drinking.

ALL-GRAIN VERSION

5 pounds (2.3 kg) rye malt
1 pound (454 g) Munich malt
1 pound (454 g) homemade crystal malt
1 pound (454 g) 60°L German crystal malt
4 pounds (1.8 kg) pale malt

Mash-in grains at 148°F (64°C) and hold for 90 minutes. Sparge at 170°F (77°C) and collect 5½ gallons (21 L) runoff. Proceed with recipe.

SAHTI

—

Sahti is the traditional beer of southern Finland, a rye and barley ale flavored with juniper.
Like many other indigenous beers, it traditionally is supposed to be consumed
uncarbonated before fermentation is complete. Our version uses both homemade
malts and homegrown juniper.

YIELD: 5 GALLONS (19 L) • INITIAL GRAVITY: 1.038–1.042 • FINAL GRAVITY: 1.004–1.010

1/2 pound (227 g) homemade crystal malt

1/2 pound (227 g) homemade roasted malt

3/4 pound (340 g) rye malt

6–8 inch (15–20 cm) juniper branch

3.3 pounds (1.5 kg) BierKeller light malt extract syrup

1 pound (454 g) dark brown sugar

1 tablespoon (15 ml) juniper berries

1/4 ounce (7 g) Saaz hops

1 packet Nottingham ale yeast or Wyeast 1028 London ale

1/2 cup (120 ml) corn sugar for priming

1. Pour 1 gallon (4 L) boiling water over the crushed malts and juniper branch. Allow to sit overnight, then strain and rinse with 1/2 gallon (2 L) 170°F (77°C) water.

2. Add extract and brown sugar and bring to a boil. Add the juniper berries and 1/4 ounce (7g) Saaz hops and boil 1 hour.

3. Strain hot wort into a fermenter containing 1 1/2 gallons (6 L) of chilled water. Rinse with 1/2 gallon (2 L) boiled water. Top up to 5 gallons (19 L).

4. Pitch yeast when wort cools to 70°F (21°C).

5. Ferment at ale temperatures (65 to 70°F, 18 to 21°C). Bottle with priming sugar when fermentation ceases (1 to 2 weeks).

6. Age 3 weeks before drinking.

ALL-GRAIN VERSION

5 pounds (2.3 kg) 2-row pale malt

2 pounds (908 g) homemade crystal malt

1 pound (454 g) rye malt

1/2 pound (227 g) roasted barley

Boil 7 gallons of water with juniper branch for 30 minutes. Mash-in malts at 104°F (40°C). Raise temperature to 130°F (54°C) and hold for 30 minutes. Raise temperature to 148°F (64°C) and hold for 120 minutes. Raise temperature to 172°F (78°C) for 15 minutes. Sparge at 190°F (88°C) and collect 5 gallons (19 L) runoff. Proceed with recipe.

SORGHUM ALE

Sorghum beer is the favorite drink of the indigenous population of South Africa, outselling Western style beers about seven to one. Our version is frothy and refreshingly tart.

YIELD: 1 GALLON (4 L) • INITIAL GRAVITY: 1.058–1.064 • FINAL GRAVITY: 1.015–1.018

5 pounds (2.3 kg) sorghum malt

1/2 pound (227 g) raw sorghum

1/2 pound (227 g) millet or flaked corn

1/2 pound (227 g) sorghum syrup

1 packet Whitbread ale yeast or Wyeast 1028 London ale

1/4 cup (60 ml) corn sugar for priming

1. Crush the malt. Add 1 gallon (4 L) boiling water. Stir the mash well. Add the raw sorghum and let it sit overnight, covered, to sour.

2. Drain off the sweet liquor and add 1 gallon (4 L) more boiling water to the mash. Drain off the additional sweet liquor. There should be 1½ to 1¾ gallons (6–7 L) of runoff.

3. Bring the runoff to a boil and add the millet or flaked corn and syrup. Boil for approximately 3 hours, until only 1-gallon (3.8 L) of wort is left.

4. Pour the wort into a fermenter (a sanitized milk jug makes a nice 1-gallon (4 L) fermenter; a size 6½ stopper fits the neck exactly).

5. Pitch the yeast when wort cools to 70°F (21°C).

6. Ferment at 60 to 70°F (15 to 21°C). Although usually consumed before it has finished fermenting, you can also bottle sorghum ale with priming sugar. This ale keeps a long time when bottled.

SPELTBIER

Speltbier is a Dutch beer from the seventeenth century, brewed from double-mashed spelt and a variety of other grains. Our ale, based on Seattle-based Big Time Brewery's version, is a nearly opaque copper color, spicy with hops, and piquant.

YIELD: 5 GALLONS (19 L) • INITIAL GRAVITY: 1.055–1.060 • FINAL GRAVITY: 1.038–1.040

- 3/4 pound (340 g) Munich malt
- 1/4 pound (112 g) toasted malt
- 1/2 pound (227 g) homemade crystal malt
- 1/3 pound (150 g) wheat malt
- 1/3 pound (150 g) rye malt
- 1/3 pound (150 g) steel-cut oats
- 1/2 pound (227 g) spelt malt
- 3.3 pounds (1.5 kg) Northwest amber malt extract syrup
- 2 pounds (908 g) dry wheat malt extract
- 2 ounces (55 g) Saaz hops for bittering, AA 5%, HBU 10
- 1 ounce (28 g) Hallertauer hops for bittering, AA 5%, HBU 5
- 1 ounce (28 g) Saaz hops for aroma
- 1 ounce (28 g) Styrian Goldings whole hops
- Yeastlab A08 Belgian ale yeast
- 3/4 cup (180 g) corn sugar for priming

1. Add the crushed malts to 2 gallons (7.5 L) cold water. Bring to a slow boil over 30 minutes. Strain and rinse with ½ gallon (2 L) 170°F (77°C) water.
2. Add extracts and return to a boil. Boil 20 minutes. Add 2 ounces (55 g) Saaz and 1 ounce (28 g) Hallertauer bittering hops and boil 40 minutes. Add 1 ounce (28 g) Saaz aroma hops to the final 2 minutes of boil.
3. Strain the hot wort into a fermenter containing 1½ gallons (6 L) of chilled water. Rinse hops with ½ gallon (2 L) boiled water. Top up to 5 gallons (19 L). Pitch yeast when wort cools to 70°F (21°C).
4. Ferment at ale temperatures (65 to 70°F, 18 to 21°C). When primary fermentation slows, add 1 ounce (28 g) Styrian Goldings dry hops.
5. Bottle when fermentation ceases (4 to 6 weeks).

ALL-GRAIN VERSION

- 3 pounds (1.3 kg) pale malt
- 2 pounds (908 g) Munich malt
- 1½ pounds (680 g) toasted malt
- 1 pound (454 g) homemade crystal malt
- 1 pound (454 g) wheat malt
- 1 pound (454 g) rye malt
- 3/4 pound (340 g) steel-cut oats
- 3/4 pound (340 g) spelt malt

Mash-in grains at 151°F (66°C). Hold for 90 minutes and sparge at 168°F (76°C). Collect 5½ gallons (21 L) of runoff.

SPRUCE BEER

Spruce beer was brewed during the American Revolution as a tonic for the troops, but it was a crude, molasses-based beverage with a strong piney flavor. This version is much more palatable, with spruce and molasses accents to recall its historic ancestry.

Some brewers recommend the use of spruce essence in beer, but we'd rather use the real thing. Spruce essence is too strong except in minute doses, and you can easily end up with a beer that tastes like turpentine.

YIELD: 5 GALLONS (19 L) • INITIAL GRAVITY: 1.045–1.050 • FINAL GRAVITY: 1.012–1.018

½ pound (227 g) homemade crystal malt
⅓ pound (150 g) homemade roasted malt
⅓ pound (150 g) chocolate malt
¼ pound (112 g) rye malt
¼ pound (112 g) black patent malt
6 pounds (2.7 kg) Northwest dark malt extract syrup
½ cup (120 ml) molasses
2 ounces (55 g) Hallertauer hops for bittering, AA 5%, HBU 10
1–4 ounces (28–112 g) spruce tips
1 packet Whitbread ale yeast
⅔ cup (160 ml) corn sugar for priming

1. Add the crushed malts to 1½ gallons (6 L) cold water and bring to a slow boil over 30 minutes. Strain and rinse with ½ gallon (2 L) 170°F (77°C) water. Add the extract and molasses and return the mixture to a boil.

2. Add 2 ounces (56 g) Hallertauer hops and spruce. Boil 60 minutes.

3. Strain hot wort into a fermenter containing 1½ gallons (6 L) of chilled water. Rinse with ½ gallon (2 L) boiled water. Top up to 5 gallons (19 L). Pitch yeast when wort cools to 70°F (21°C).

4. Ferment at ale temperatures (65 to 70°F, 18 to 21°C). Bottle with priming sugar when fermentation ceases (1 to 2 weeks).

5. Age 3 to 6 weeks before drinking.

ALL-GRAIN VERSION

1½ pounds (680 g) home-made crystal malt
½ pound (227 g) roasted barley
3 pounds (1.3 kg) rye malt
6 pounds (2.7 kg) pale malt
½ pound (227 g) black patent malt

Mash-in the grains with 3½ gallons (13 L) 148°F (64°C) water and hold for 2 hours. Sparge at 170°F (77°C) and collect 5½ gallons (21 L) runoff. Proceed with recipe.

DANDELION STOUT

Dandelion Stout sold here at 2d. a bottle.

— Sign over a shop in the Midlands, England, circa 1910

YIELD: 5 GALLONS (19 L) • INITIAL GRAVITY: 1.065–1.070 • FINAL GRAVITY: 1.013–1.019

1/3 pound (150 g) black patent malt

2/3 pound (300 g) 60°L British crystal malt

1/2 pound (227 g) chocolate malt

1/3 pound (150 g) roasted barley

1/3 pound (150 g) wheat malt

4 pounds (1.8 kg) Alexander's hopped malt extract syrup

3.3 pounds (1.5 kg) Northwest dark malt extract syrup

3/4 pound (340 g) Munton & Fison plain light dry malt extract

1 pound (454 g) dandelions

1/2 ounce (14 g) Eroica bittering hops, AA 11%, HBU 5.5

1/2 ounce (14 g) homegrown Cascade flavoring hops

1 packet Whitbread ale yeast or YeastLab A05 Irish Ale

1/2 cup (120 ml) corn sugar for priming

1. Clean the dandelions very thoroughly in several changes of water, removing any twigs or other debris.

2. Add the crushed malts to 1½ gallons (6 L) cold water and bring to a slow boil over 30 minutes. Strain and rinse with ½ gallon (2 L) 170°F (77°C) water. Add the extracts and return the mixture to a boil.

3. Add ½ ounce (14 g) Eroica hops and dandelions. Boil 40 minutes. Add ½ ounce (14 g) Cascade hops and boil 20 minutes.

4. Strain hot wort into a fermenter containing 1½ gallons (6 L) of chilled water. Rinse with ½ gallon (2 L) boiled water. Top up to 5 gallons (19 L). Pitch yeast when wort cools to 70°F (21°C).

5. Ferment at ale temperatures (65 to 70°F, 18 to 21°C). Bottle with priming sugar when fermentation ceases (1 to 2 weeks).

6. Age 3 to 6 weeks before drinking.

ALL-GRAIN VERSION

7 pounds (3 kg) Klages malt

1 pound (454 g) Munich malt

1 pound (454 g) wheat malt

1¼ pounds (560 g) 60°L British crystal malt

1 pound (454 g) roasted barley

1/2 pound (227 g) black patent malt

Mash-in grains, stabilize at 153°F (67°C), and hold 90 minutes. Sparge at 170°F (77°C) and collect 5½ gallons (21 L) runoff. Proceed with recipe.

SORGHUM FOREIGN EXTRA STOUT

Guinness makes a "foreign" extra stout in South Africa using the favored local sorghum as an ingredient. It adds an interesting quirkiness to the familiar dark brew.

YIELD: 5 GALLONS (19 L) • INITIAL GRAVITY: 1.087 (EXTRACT), 1.125 (ALL GRAIN) • FINAL GRAVITY: 1.015–1.021

$^3/_4$ pound (340 g) 60°L British crystal malt

$^1/_2$ pound (227 g) chocolate malt

$^1/_3$ pound (150 g) Munich malt

$^1/_3$ pound (150 g) homemade roasted malt

$^1/_3$ pound (150 g) black patent malt

3 pounds (1.3 kg) dry amber spray malt

$^1/_3$ pound (150 g) sorghum malt or raw sorghum

6 pounds (2.7 kg) Northwest dark malt extract

$^1/_2$ pound (227 g) dry wheat malt extract

1 pound (454 g) sorghum syrup

2 ounces (55 g) Eroica flavoring hops, AA 11%, HBU 22

1 ounce (28 g) Cascade flavoring hops, AA 6%, HBU 6

YeastLab A05 Irish Ale

$^1/_2$ cup (120 ml) corn sugar or for priming

1. Crush the raw sorghum and boil 30 minutes in 1 gallon (2 L) water. Add the crushed malts. Stabilize at 150°F (65°C) and hold for 30 minutes. Strain and rinse with $^1/_2$ gallon (2 L) 170°F (77°C) water.

2. Add the extracts and sorghum syrup. Add Eroica hops and boil 40 minutes. Add Cascade hops and boil 20 minutes.

3. Strain hot wort into a fermenter containing 1$^1/_2$ gallons (6 L) of chilled water. Rinse with $^1/_2$ gallon (2 L) boiled water. Top up to 5 gallons (19 L).

4. Pitch yeast when wort cools to 70°F (21°C).

5. Ferment at ale temperatures (65 to 70°F, 18 to 21°C). Bottle when fermentation ceases (1 to 2 weeks).

6. Age 3 to 6 weeks before drinking.

ALL-GRAIN VERSION

10 pounds (4.5 kg) Klages malt

2 pounds (908 g) Munich malt

1 pound (454 g) roasted barley

3 pounds (1.3 kg) unmalted sorghum

$^3/_4$ pound (350 g) chocolate malt

1$^1/_2$ pounds (680 g) crystal malt

$^1/_2$ pound (227 g) wheat malt

Boil sorghum 30 minutes with 3$^1/_2$ gallons (1 L) water. Mash-in malts, stabilize at 122°F (50°C), and hold for 30 minutes. Raise to 153°F (67°C) and hold 45 minutes. Sparge at 170°F (77°C) and collect 6 gallons (23 L) runoff.

BJARNI'S BASIC MEAD

YIELD: 5 GALLONS (19 L) • INITIAL GRAVITY: 1.120–1.130 • FINAL GRAVITY: 1.020–1.035

> 15 pounds (6.8 kg) honey
> 1½ gallons (6 L) water
> 1 tablespoon (15 ml) gypsum
> ½ ounce (14 g) yeast nutrient
> 1 packet champagne yeast

1. Place all the ingredients except the yeast in a large pot and boil for 10 to 15 minutes. Pour into a carboy containing a gallon of chilled water. Top off with more water to make 5 gallons (19 L).
2. When the wort has cooled to 75°F (24°C), pitch the yeast. Ferment between 65 to 70°F (18 to 21°C). Mead can easily take a year to ferment completely, and sometimes up to five. We've had a batch of raspberry mead in the cellar for three years now, and we are in no hurry to bottle it.

ADDING FRUIT TO MEAD

To create a special treat, add 6 to 10 pounds of berries to your mead mixture just after the 15-minute boil. Do not strain the berries before fermentation.

HARD CIDER

Unless you have several trees, you probably won't have enough apples to make much cider. Also, the best cider is made from a combination of different apples rather than by using just one variety. We have an annual ritual in which we get together with a group of other local homebrewers for mass pressing. We let an apple farm know in advance when we are coming, and they put together a nice mix of cider apples for us, mostly Baldwins with a few other varieties. We have not tried a commercial cider yet which is comparable in quality to what we brew ourselves.

YIELD: 5 GALLONS (19 L) • INITIAL GRAVITY: 1.070 • FINAL GRAVITY: 1.008–1.010

> 3 pounds (1.4 kg) honey
> 2 Campden tablets (potassium metabisulfate), crushed
> 5 gallons (19 L) of sweet apple cider
> 1–2 packets of champagne yeast

1. Melt 3 pounds (1.4 kg) of honey over low heat with about 1 gallon (4 L) of cider. Reserve one pint of this mixture in a sanitized canning jar with a rubber-sealed lid. Put the sealed jar in boiling water for 10 minutes to pasteurize. Set aside this jar in the refrigerator. It will be used later as a priming solution at bottling time.

2. Pour the remaining 4 gallons (15 L) of cider into a glass carboy. Add the rest of the honey/cider solution to the carboy.

3. Add 2 crushed Campden tablets (potassium metabisulfate) to the carboy and seal it with a fermentation lock for 24 hours. That will inhibit the activity of any wild yeasts or *Acetobacter* (mother of vinegar microbes) that may be in the cider. If you're allergic to sulfites, reduce the amount of sterilizer you use. You won't be able to detect one tablet dissolved in 5 gallons (19 L) of cider. The 24-hour wait will allow the sulfur dioxide from the potassium metabisulfate to clear and make the cider safe for your yeast.

4. Pitch a packet or two of champagne yeast in your carboy. Let yeast get a start at room temperature (65 to 70°F, 18 to 21°C) then move carboy to cellar temperature to finish fermenting (40° to 50°F, 4° to 10°C).

5. Cider usually takes a few months before it is ready to bottle, at which point you boil the pint of unfermented cider and add it to the bottling bucket.

6. Bottle the cider. Hard cider kept a year in the bottle turns into a splendid sparkling beverage that, to our humble palates, tastes better than any champagne.

PERRY

—

Perry can be described as pear cider, or pear wine. Like cider, the best perry is produced with a mix of pears having different characteristics. Perry is produced by two separate fermentations: a yeast fermentation, followed by a malic acid fermentation brought on by wild bacteria.

YIELD: 5 GALLONS (19 L) • INITIAL GRAVITY: 1.065–1.070 • FINAL GRAVITY: 1.008–1.010

> 100 **pounds (45 kg) pears**
> 2¹/₂ **Campden tablets (potassium metabisulfate), crushed**
> 1 **teaspoon (5 ml) malic acid (if necessary)**
> 1 **teaspoon (5 ml) calcium carbonate (if necessary)**
> **Honey (if necessary)**
> 1 **packet Red Star Champagne yeast or YeastLab A04 British ale yeast**

1. Pick the pears when they are fully ripe, but not overripe. Store them in a cool, dark place to mature for 2 to 7 days. This period is critical to good perry; if the pears are too green, little juice can be extracted from them, with little flavor. If they are left too long, they will begin to rot. Pulp the pears (the grinder on a cider press or a fruit mill is useful for this) and place them in covered, sanitized plastic buckets overnight in a cool place, to express their juices and tannin.

2. Press in a cider or wine press to extract the juice. Use a sanitized plastic bucket to catch the juice and pour it into a carboy. Test the pH and take a hydrometer reading. The pH should be 3.5 to 4.0. To lower the pH, add malic acid (but not citric acid; citric acid fermentation will ruin the perry). To raise it, add calcium carbonate. If the specific gravity is too low, add a pound or so of honey (see cider recipe).

3. Add Campden tablets and seal the carboy. Don't be concerned about killing the malic acid microbes; the sulfur will only slow them down. Wait 24 hours and pitch yeast.

4. After 4 weeks or so, rack the perry off to a secondary fermenter. Let yeast get a start at room temperature (65 to 70°F, 18 to 21°C) then move carboy to cellar temperature to finish fermenting (40° to 50°F, 4° to 10°C). Fermentation should be complete in another 4 to 6 weeks. Bottle, but do not prime. Perries are usually served still, and carbonation increases the chance of an acetic acid reaction and a spoiled batch.

5. Store the perry for at least 3 months before drinking. Fresh perry tastes like fresh cider; mature is smoother and milder, with almost butterscotch notes from the malo-lactic acid fermentation.

Appendix A

Measurements and Conversions

Three measuring systems — United States, Imperial (British), and Metric — confuse the homebrewing world. Here are a few basic rules to help you make sense of it all.

Liquid Measures

1 U.S. gallon = 3.8 liters
1 U.S. gallon = .833 Imperial gallons
1 Imperial gallon = 1.2 U.S. gallons
5 U.S. gallons = 1.9 liters
5 U.S. gallons = 4.165 Imperial gallons
1 Imperial pint = 20 ounces
1 U.S. pint = 2 cups = 473 milliliters
1 U.S. quart = 950 milliliters

Dry Measures

½ teaspoon = 2.5 milliliters
1 teaspoon = 5 milliliters
2 teaspoons = 10 milliliters
1 tablespoon = 15 milliliters
¼ cup = 60 milliliters
⅓ cup = 80 milliliters
½ cup = 120 milliliters
1 cup = 230 milliliters

Temperature

Degrees Celsius = 5/9 (Fahrenheit − 32)
Degrees Fahrenheit = (9/5 × Celsius) + 32

Weight

¼ ounce = 7 grams
½ ounce = 14 grams
1 ounce = 28 grams
¼ pound = 112 grams
½ pound = 227 grams
¾ pound = 340 grams
1 pound = 454 grams
1½ pounds = 680 grams
2 pounds = 908 grams
3 pounds = 1.3 kilograms
3.3 pounds = 1.5 kilograms
4 pounds = 1.8 kilograms
5 pounds = 2.3 kilograms
6 pounds = 2.7 kilograms

Length

1 inch = 25 millimeters or
   2.5 centimeters

Appendix B

Sources for Garden and Brewing Supplies

Seeds

The last ten years have seen a boom in specialty seed catalogs and in organizations like the Seed Savers Exchange, which is dedicated to finding, preserving, and distributing heirloom varieties. This gives the homebrewer a lot of avenues when trying to locate seeds for unusual brewing herbs or other beer ingredients. Membership is not expensive, and you get to help preserve unusual brewing herbs and grains that might eventually disappear otherwise.

Abundant Life Seed Company
541-767-9606
www.abundantlifeseeds.com

Bountiful Gardens
707-459-6410
www.bountifulgardens.org

Fedco Seeds
207-873-7333
www.fedcoseeds.com

Irish Eyes — Garden City Seeds
509-964-7000
www.gardencityseeds.net

J. L Hudson, Seedsman
inquiry@jlhudsonseeds.net
www.jlhudsonseeds.com

Johnny's Selected Seeds
877-564-6697
www.johnnyseeds.com

Peters Seed and Research
seed@psrseed.com
www.psrseed.com

Pinetree Garden Seeds
207-926-3400
www.superseeds.com

R. H. Shumway's
800-342-9461
www.rhshumway.com

Seeds of Change
888-762-7333
www.seedsofchange.com

Seed Savers Exchange
563-382-5990
www.seedsavers.org
Not a seed company but a genetic preservation
project. The members exchange rare flower, herb,
garlic and potato seeds for a nominal fee.

Herb Plants

Artistic Gardens & Le Jardin du Gourmet
802-748-1446
www.artisticgardens.com

Edible Landscaping
800-524-4156
www.eat-it.com

Gurney's Seed & Nursery Co.
513-354-1491
www.gurneys.com

Heaths & Heathers Nursery
800-294-3284
www.heathsandheathers.com

Henry Field's Seed & Nursery Co.
513-354-1494
www.henryfields.com

Jung Quality Seeds
800-297-3123
www.jungseed.com

Richters Herbs
905-640-6677
www.richters.com

Grain

Rupp Seeds Inc.
419-337-1841
www.ruppseeds.com

Sustainable Seed Company
877-620-7333
www.sustainableseedco.com

Welter Seed & Honey Co.
800-728-8450
www.welterseed.com

Tree Seeds

F.W. Schumacher Co., Inc.
508-888-0659
www.treeshrubseeds.com

Miller Nurseries
800-836-9630
www.millernurseries.com

Hop Rhizomes

Beer and Wine Makers of America
408-441-0880
www.beerandwinemakers.com

Freshops
800-460-6925
www.freshops.com

Nichols Garden Nursery
800-422-3985
www.nicholsgardennursery.com

Garden Tools

A. M. Leonard
800-543-8955
www.amleo.com

Alternative Garden Supply
800-444-2837
www.altgarden.com

Gempler's
800-382-8473
www.gemplers.com

Kinsman Company
800-733-4146
www.kinsmangarden.com

Worm's Way
800-274-9676
www.wormsway.com

Organic Pest and Disease Solutions

Gardens Alive!
513-354-1482
www.gardensalive.com

Snow Pond Farm Supply
781-878-5581
www.snow-pond.com

Homebrew Supplies

Austin Homebrew Supply
800-890-2739
www.austinhomebrew.com

Bacchus and Barleycorn, Ltd.
913-962-2501
www.bacchus-barleycorn.com

Beer & Wine Hobby
781-933-8818
www.beer-wine.com

The Beverage People
800-544-1867
www.thebeveragepeople.com

Country Wines
412-366-0151
www.countrywines.com

DeFalco's
800-216-2739
www.defalcos.com

E. C. Kraus
800-353-1906
www.eckraus.com

Fermenter's International Trade Association
(Formerly Home Wine and Beer Trade Association)
330-633-7223
www.fermentersinternational.org

Grape and Granary
800-695-9870
www.grapeandgranary.com

The Home Brewery
800-321-2739
www.homebrewery.com

Just Brew It!
(Formerly Aardvark Brewing Supplies)
770-719-0222
www.justbrewit-ga.com

Midwest Homebrewing Supplies
888-449-2739
www.midwestsupplies.com

Seven Bridges Cooperative
800-768-4409
www.breworganic.com
Specializes in organic beer
supplies.

William's Brewing Company
800-759-6025
www.williamsbrewing.com

WindRiver Brewing Company
800-266-4677
www.windriverbrew.com

Glossary

AA: See *Alpha acids*

Acetobacter: Vinegar-producing bacteria.

Acrospire: The first leaf, or sprout, of a grain of barley.

Adjuncts: Fermentable beer ingredients other than malted barley. These include corn, rice, wheat, oats, and rye.

Ale: Style of beer produced by top-fermenting yeast strains at warm temperatures. Originated in the British Isles. Includes bitter, stout, porter, India Pale Ale, and others.

Alpha acids (AA): The acids that form the main bittering agents in hops. The alpha acid percentage is derived by multiplying the amount of alpha acid in a given sample of hops by its weight in ounces.

Annual: A plant that completes its entire life cycle in one year. *Hardy annuals* can withstand quite a bit of frost, often overwintering as self-sown seeds. *Half-hardy annuals* can withstand light frost but are killed by repeated exposure to cold. *Frost-tender annuals* are tropical plants; they can be killed even by light frost.

Aroma hops: Hops added at the end of the boil to contribute delicate hop aromas to the beer. Sometimes called finishing hops. Hallertauer, Saaz, and Willamette are three varieties that are often used as aroma hops.

Barley: A cereal grain, the seeds of which (barleycorns) are used in making beer. There are different varieties, 2-row and 6-row, which impart different qualities to the beer.

Biennial: A plant with a two-year life cycle. It produces only leaves the first year, flowering and dying the second year.

Bolting: Very rapid growth, especially of flowering stalks. In the malting process, uncontrolled acrospire growth.

Bracteoles: Petal-like parts of hop cone; they contain the lupulin glands and seeds.

Bracts: Hop cone "petals" without lupulin glands.

Broadcasting: Scattering seed evenly over the ground.

Burr: Early phase in the development of the hop cones, before the *bracts* and *bracteoles* appear.

Butanol: Poisonous form of alcohol produced by bacterial fermentation (also used as a solvent).

Butryfying bacteria: Organisms that produce butanol.

Campden tablets: Tablets of potassium metabisulafte used to inhibit infection in wine, cider, and mead.

Carboy: A 5- to 6½-gallon, clear glass bottle that can be used as a fermenting vessel.

Cold frame: Boxlike structure with a clear glass lid and no bottom, used to protect plants from cold.

Cold treatment: Exposing seeds to low temperatures to enhance germination. Only required for some seeds.

Couching: The stage of malting following germination, in which oxygen is withheld from the grain to allow enzymatic modification of starches to take place.

Cultivar: A named variety of plant, either hybrid or open pollinated. From "*culti*vated *vari*ety."

Damping-off: Fungal disease that causes young seedlings to rot at the soil line and fall over.

Diatomaceous earth: Dust composed of the broken shells of tiny sea creatures used to kill insect pests by dehydration.

Dry hopping: Addition of whole hops (or herbs) to beer during secondary fermentation to enhance aroma.

Fermentation: The stage of the yeast's life cycle following reproduction, during which it eats malt sugars and produces alcohol, carbon dioxide, and some flavors of beer.

Fermentation lock: Plastic valve that vents carbon dioxide from the fermentation vessel without letting in any outside air. It prevents contamination of beer by microbes.

Finishing hops: See *aroma hops*

Frost-free date: The date of the last expected frost in spring. This is the first day it's safe to plant tender annual plants in your area. If you're not sure, ask your local Cooperative Extension Service.

Fusarium wilt: A fungal disease of tomatoes that can also infect hops. It causes withering of hop leaves.

Germination: The sprouting of a seed. In the malting process, the sprouting of the grain transforms stored starches into sugars suitable for brewing.

Green malt: Wet, finished malt that hasn't been kilned yet.

Hardening off: Gradually acclimatizing plants that have been grown indoors to outside conditions.

Hardiness: The amount of cold a perennial plant can tolerate, as described by the USDA Hardiness Zone map (see page 61). For hardy annuals and hardy biennials, see under *Annual.*

HBU: See *Home Bittering Units*

Herb: A plant grown for its flavoring or medicinal properties. In brewing, any plant besides hops that is used to flavor or bitter beer.

Home Bittering Units (HBU): Unit of potential bitterness in a given amount of hops per volume of beer. HBU = alpha acid content (percent) × number of ounces of bittering hops.

Hop yard: The field or bed in which hops are grown.

Hybrid: Plant that is the offspring of genetically dissimilar parent plants. Hybrid varieites are often more vigorous. But unlike open-pollinated varieties, you can't save their seeds and expect to get similar plants.

Insecticidal soap: Soap sprays used to kill insect pests through dehydration and suffocation.

International Bitterness Units (IBU): System of measuring hop bitterness used in the brewing industry. 1 IBU = 1 milligram of isomerized alpha acid dissolved in 1 liter of wort or beer.

Invasive: Describing plants that tend to take over, either by runners, rhizomes, or agressive self-sowing. Mints are a good example of invasive plants.

Jora: South American malted corn.

Kilning: The process of drying the finished malt at low temperatures.

Krausen: High-foaming head that forms on beer during primary fermentation.

Lager: Style of beer produced by bottom-fermenting yeasts at low temperatures. Originated in Germany. Includes Maëzens, bocks, and Oktoberfests, among others.

Loam: Ideal garden soil. Medium-textured, easily worked soil made up of equal parts sand, silt, and clay. Usually high in organic matter.

Lovibond: System of measuring beer color based on the color that 1 pound of malt will contribute to 1 U.S. gallon of beer. Recently replaced by Standard Reference Method (SRM). Measured in degrees.

Lupulin: Yellow, resinous powder found in hop cones. It contains alpha and beta acids as well as other characteristic hop chemicals.

Malt: Cereal grain (generally barley, but not always) that has been partially germinated, dried, and/or roasted to produce different brewing characteristics. Malt varieties include pale malt, crystal malt, black patent malt, chocolate malt, Vienna malt, and others.

Malt extract: Concentrated wort in syrup or powder form. Can be hopped or unhopped.

Malting: The process of turning raw grain into malt suitable for brewing. The entire malting process consists of steeping, germination, couching, kilning, and roasting.

Malting barley: Barley that has been bred specifically for brewing. Can be either 2-row or 6-row.

Mashing: The process of extracting sweet liquor from malted grains by means of temperature-controlled steeping.

Open-pollinated: A plant that produces offspring with the same genetic characteristics. If a variety is open-pollinated, you can save its seeds and expect to get similar plants from them (the seedlings will resemble the parent plants). See also *Hybrids*.

Perennial: A plant with a life cycle lasting many years. It either dies back to the ground in winter, or maintains a woody aboveground structure.

Pitching: Adding yeast to cooled wort.

Primary fermentation: The first, very active phase of fermentation. It proceeds from the time of pitching until the krausen drops, including the respiration and reproduction stages of the yeast's life cycle.

Priming: The process of adding sugar or malt extract to beer at bottling time. The yeast in the bottled beer digest this sugar and produce carbon dioxide to induce carbonation in the finished beer.

Racking: The process of siphoning unfinished homebrew from the primary fermentation vessel to another vessel such as a carboy.

Reinheitsgebot: German law enacted in 1516 forbidding the use of any ingredients but malt, hops, and yeast in beer.

Rhizome: Underground runners by which plants such as hops and mints spread themselves. Rhizome cuttings are the usual means of propagating hops.

Roasting: The process of converting kilned pale malt into specialty brewing malt by subjecting it to high temperatures.

Rosa solis: Mixture of different herbs used in sixteenth century brewing.

Runoff: See *Sweet liquor*

Scratch brewing: Brewing using as many homegrown or self-produced ingredients as possible. Ideally, it refers to all-grain brewing using only homegrown malt and hops.

Self-sowing: Referring to annual plants that reappear every year on their own by distributing their own seeds. Many plants, such as borage, come back year after year from self-sowing.

Sparging: The process of rinsing residual sugars from mashed grains with boiled water.

Spp.: Abbreviation for species. Used in botanical names to refer to more than one species.

Steeping: The first part of the malting process, in which grain is soaked in water prior to germination.

Strig: The central stem of a hop cone.

Sweet liquor: The liquid produced from all-grain mashing. Also called runoff.

Tent training: Trellising hops up guy wires attacked to a central pole.

Threshing: Breaking harvested grains free from their dried seedheads.

Transplanting: Removing a plant from the container in which it has been grown and replanting it in the ground.

Trellis: Support structure for growing hops or other vines.

Verticillium wilt: A fungal disease of tomatoes which effects hops by withering their leaves.

Winnowing: Separating harvested grains from chaff and dried plant debris by pouring them back and forth in a light breeze.

Wort: Unfermented beer.

Bibliography and Suggested Reading

Aaronson, Wendy and Bill Ridgely. "Adventures in Chicha and Chang: Indigenous Beers of the East and West." *Zymurgy* 17, no. 1 (1994): 32.

Ashworth, Suzanne. *Seed to Seed*. Decorah, IA: Seed Saver Publications, 1991.

Beach, David R. *Homegrown Hops: An Illustrated How-to-Do-It Manual*. Self-published, 1988.

Cantwell, Dick. "Brew Art History — Dutch Brewing in the Seventeenth Century." *Zymurgy* 17, no. 2 (1994): 32.

Dale, R. C. "Home Malting for Homebrewers." *Zymurgy* 8, no. 4, (1985): 17.

Eames, Alan D. *The Secret Life of Beer!: Legends, Lore & Little-Known Facts*. North Adams, MA: Storey Publishing, 2005.

Fisher, Joe and Dennis Fisher. *Great Beer from Kits*. North Adams, MA: Storey Publishing, 1996.

Garetz, Mark. *Using Hops: the Complete Guide to Hops for the Craft Brewer*. Danville, CA: HopTech, 1994.

Hall, Dorothy. *The Book of Herbs*. New York: Charles Scribner's Sons, 1972.

Hart, Rhonda Massingham. *Dirt-Cheap Gardening*. North Adams, MA: Storey Publishing, 1995.

Jackson, Michael. *Beer Companion*. Philadelphia, PA: Running Press, 1993.

Jacobs, Betty E. M. *Growing & Using Herbs Successfully*. North Adams, MA: Storey Publishing, 1981.

Jason, Dan. "Amaranth: Ancient Grain, Modern Greens." *Organic Gardening Magazine*, Vol. 40, no. 4 (1993): 40.

Kowlachik, Claire and William H. Hylton, eds. *Rodale's Illustrated Encyclopedia of Herbs*. Emmaus, PA: Rodale Press, 1987.

La Pensee, Clive. *The Historical Companion to House-Brewing*. Beverly, U.K.: Montag Publications, 1990.

Loewer, Peter. *Tough Plants for Tough Places*. Emmaus, PA: Rodale Press, 1992.

Logson, Gene. *Small-Scale Grain Raising*. Emmaus, PA: Rodale Press, 1977.

Lundgren, Hakan. "Gotlandsdrika, the Ancient Brew of Gotland." *Zymurgy* 17, no. 4 (1994): 9.

Lutzen, Karl F. and Mark Stevens. *Homebrew Favorites*. North Adams, MA: Storey Publishing, 1994.

McClure, Susan. *The Herb Gardener: A Guide for All Seasons*. North Adams, MA: Storey Publishing, 1996.

Mosher, Randy. *The Brewer's Companion*. Seattle, WA: Alephenalia Publications, 1994.

Papazian, Charlie. *The Homebrewer's Companion*. New York: Avon Books, 1994.

Proulx, Annie and Lew Nichols. *Cider: Making, Using, & Enjoying Sweet and Hard Cider*. North Adams, MA: Storey Publishing, 1997.

Ridgely, Bill. "African Sorghum Beer." *Zymurgy* 17, no. 4 (1994): 28.

Rupp, Rebecca. *Red Oaks & Black Birches: The Science and Lore of Trees*. North Adams, MA: Storey Publishing, 1990.

Samuels, Mary. "Quinoa — Grain of the '90s." *Zymurgy* 17, no. 4 (1994): 90.

Schaefer, Mike. "Sahti: A Traditional Finnish Brew." *Zymurgy* 17, no. 4 (1994): 6.

Seymour, John. *The Guide to Self-Sufficency*. New York: Popular Mechanics Books, 1976.

Smith, Gregg. *The Beer Enthusiast's Guide*. North Adams, MA: Storey Publishing, 1994.

Turcotte, Patricia. *The New England Herb Gardener*. Woodstock, VT: The Countryman Press, 1990.

Vargas, Pattie and Rich Gulling. *Country Wines: Making & Using Wines from Herbs, Fruits, Flowers, & More*. North Adams, MA: Storey Publishing, 1992.

Williams, Bruce. "Leann Fraoch — Scottish Heather Ale." *Zymurgy* 17, no. 4 (1994): 24.

Wood, Heather. *The Beer Directory: An International Guide*. North Adams, MA: Storey Publishing, 1995.

Index

Note: **Boldface** entries indicate recipes. Page numbers in *italic* indicate illustrations; page numbers in boldface indicate tables.

Other Storey Titles You Will Enjoy

Brew Ware: How to Find, Adapt & Build Homebrewing Equipment, by Karl F. Lutzen & Mark Stevens.
Step-by-step instructions to build tools to make brewing safer and easier.
272 pages. Paper. ISBN 978-0-88266-926-7.

CloneBrews, 2nd **edition,** by Tess and Mark Szamatulski.
One hundred and fifty recipes to brew beer that tastes just like premium commercial brands.
440 pages. Paper. ISBN 978-1-60342-539-1.

Dave Miller's Homebrewing Guide, by Dave Miller.
A simple yet complete overview of homebrewing that is clear enough for the novice but thorough enough for the brewmaster.
368 pages. Paper. ISBN 978-0-88266-905-2.

Homebrew Favorites, by Karl F. Lutzen & Mark Stevens.
Favorite recipes collected from homebrewers across North America, with straightforward directions for everything from the simple to the exotic.
256 pages. Paper. ISBN 978-0-88266-613-6.

The Homebrewer's Answer Book, by Ashton Lewis.
Hundreds of brewing problems solved by *Brew Your Own* magazine's Mr. Wizard.
432 pages. Flexibind. ISBN 978-1-58017-675-0.

North American CloneBrews, by Scott R. Russell.
Recipes to duplicate your favorite American and Canadian beers at home.
176 pages. Paper. ISBN 978-1-58017-246-2.

Tasting Beer, by Randy Mosher.
The first comprehensive guide to tasting, appreciating, and understanding the world's best drink — craft beers.
256 pages. Paper. ISBN 978-1-60342-089-1.

These and other books from Storey Publishing are available wherever quality books are sold or by calling 1-800-441-5700.
Visit us at *www.storey.com.*